REED CONCISE GUIDE

ORCHIDS
of Australia

David L Jones

First published in 2025 by Reed New Holland Publishers

newhollandpublishers.com

A record of this book is held at the National Library of Australia.

ISBN 9781760796464

Managing Director: Fiona Schultz
General Manager: Olga Dementiev
Publisher and Project Editor: Simon Papps
Designer: Andrew Davies
Production Director: Arlene Gippert

Printed in China

Keep up with Reed New Holland
and New Holland Publishers

 ReedNewHolland

@NewHollandPublishers and @ReedNewHolland

Front cover: *Thelymitra variegata* (L. Copeland).

Page 1: *Durabaculum phalaenopsis*.

Back cover (left to right): *Sarcochilus australis, Diuris aurea, Caladenia radialis*.

CONTENTS

INTRODUCTION

Orchids are an important group of monocotyledons which can be recognised by a unique set of floral features. They are a natural group of plants in which the perianth segments are in threes – three sepals and three petals which may all be alike, or differ in shape, size, colour and texture. The outer whorl of three is known as the sepals and the inner whorl is the petals. Often the sepals and petals of orchids are very similar in size, shape and colour and are then referred to as tepals. In orchids, the front petal is modified into a structure that differs from the other two petals. Known as the lip or labellum, this organ plays a major role in attracting pollinating vectors to the flower and bringing about pollination. Another notable floral feature in orchids is the fusion of the male and female sexual parts to form a structure known as the column. This organ is situated centrally in the flower and is often quite conspicuous. The male (anther) and female (stigma) sex organs are separate on the column (anther usually at the top), although they may be in close proximity.

Numbers: Orchids are the largest and most successful group of plants on Earth. A 2016 study places their number at c.27,800 species in 880 genera but those figures change regularly with the discovery, formal description and naming of new species. The greatest diversity of species and total numbers of orchids occur in the tropics, but orchids are widely distributed around the globe and are found in almost every land-based habitat. Currently, Australia has c.1,700 named species of native orchids in 156 genera, about 90 per cent of which are endemic to the continent.

Coverage: This tiny book contains 195 species of Australian native orchids in 79 genera, a small sample of the species found on this remarkable continent. Very few of the photos are mine, most were taken by my friend and colleague Lachlan Copeland who gave me free access to his collection. Many other friends also helped with photographs for which I am most grateful. Special thanks to David Banks, Gary Backhouse, Garry Brockman, Mark Clements, Chris French, Mike Harrison, Jeff Jeanes, June Niejalke, John Roberts, Ron Tunstall and Alan Stephenson. Unfortunately, individual photo captions were not possible in such a small book, but I sincerely thank all those who contributed.

Epiphytic orchids: Most of the world's orchid species grow as epiphytes on trees, enabling them to take advantage of suitable regimes of light, air movement and humidity. Epiphytes live independently, not parasitically, using the tree only for support and gaining nourishment from bird droppings, detritus and compounds leached from the bark. Many epiphytes also grow on rocks and may then be termed as lithophytes. About 14 per cent of Australian native orchids (some 239 species in 61 genera) are epiphytes.

Two growth habits are significant and easily identifiable in epiphytic orchids. In sympodial orchids the new growths are produced in stages, each successive growth hardening off before a new shoot is produced from its base. In these orchids the stems either resemble canes or are swollen into thickened storage units termed pseudobulbs. Flower spikes arise from the stem opposite a leaf or from buds near the top of the growth. By contrast in monopodial orchids, fleshy storage units, such as swollen stems and pseudobulbs are absent, and the main axis, often just a single fibrous stem, increases in length steadily each year. In these orchids new side growths can be produced from basal nodes and the flower spikes arise from the side of the main stem, often opposite a leaf.

Terrestrial orchids: Many orchid species grow in the ground as terrestrials. The vast majority of Australian orchids (86 per cent, or some 1,460 species in 95 genera) are terrestrial. Most of these are deciduous and known as resprouters because they have a dormant component in their annual growth cycle when the plants

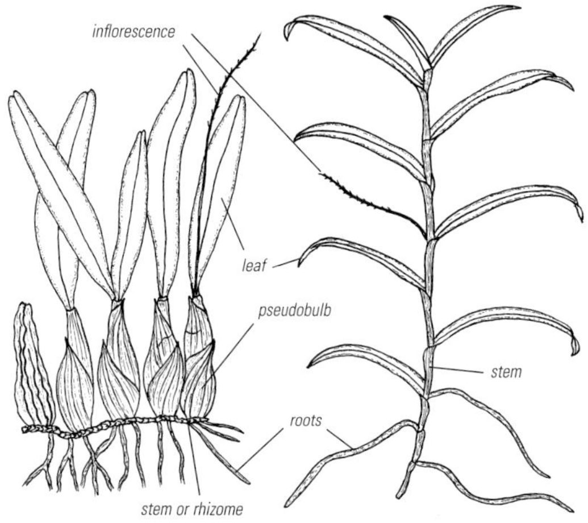

Two major growth forms of epiphytic orchids: sympodial (left), monopodial (right)

die back to a fleshy storage organ (commonly a root tuber) each year to avoid unsuitable climatic conditions (usually excessive heat and dryness), resprouting again when conditions become suitable. Most native terrestrial orchids are resprouters, few are evergreen with leaves present all year. Generally evergreen terrestrials are found in wetter tropical forests. Most terrestrial orchids grow from a single parent tuber that lasts only one season and must be replaced annually by a new tuber if the plant is to survive. As well as the replacement tuber, many native terrestrial orchids produce extra tubers each year, termed daughter tubers. These are genetically identical to the parent tuber and result in the formation of clonal colonies which can allow the orchid to spread into new areas. Some species of terrestrial orchid can produce up to five new tubers annually.

Leafless orchids: Leafless orchids lack chlorophyll, cannot photosynthesise and rely on a symbiotic relationship with fungi for their source of carbon and nutrients. Some leafless orchids, known as saprophytes, survive in a simple association with a mycorrhizal fungus in their roots and decaying wood. To survive the orchid relies entirely on the symbiotic fungus to digest decaying organic matter and transport nutrients and growth substances into their roots. *Gastrodia sesamoides* (Cinnamon Bells) is a good example of a saprophyte. Other more specialised leafless orchids, known as mycoheterotrophs, live in a three-way semiparasitic arrangement with both a specific photosynthetic host plant and a mycorrhizal fungus. The fungus forms a symbiotic relationship with the orchid, and also with the plant, transferring nutrients and growth compounds from the plant into the orchid roots. Leafless species of

Dipodium (Hyacinth Orchids) are commonly seen mycoheterotrophs which live in association with a plant belonging to the family Myrtaceae (eucalypts, bottlebrushes, paperbarks, and so on).

A small group of highly specialised epiphytic orchids have evolved to survive without leaves. The roots of these orchids contain chlorophyll and take over the role of leaves, photosynthesising when exposed to sunlight. *Taeniophyllum muelleri* (page 206) is an example of such a leafless epiphyte.

Male Orchid Dupe Wasps (*Lissopimpla excelsa*) attempting to copulate with *Cryptostylis ovata* (G. Brockman).

Pollination: Most native orchids rely on the interaction of visitors to their flowers to bring about pollination. This can be achieved in a variety of ways and is a fascinating field of study.

Simple relationships involve attracting insects to the flowers by fragrance and colour and rewarding these visits with nectar. Deceit can also be involved whereby some orchid flowers, lacking nectar in this case, mimic by shape and colour the flowers of other prominent plant groups which produce nectar as a reward. Pollination by sexual deceit (termed pseudocopulation) is found in several groups of native terrestrial orchids. Sexual deception involves the flower releasing a pheromone which mimics the sex scent of a female insect and deceives the males of that insect to attempt mating with the flower, achieving pollination in the process. Bees and wasps are the insects most commonly deceived by sexual deception, but males of tiny flies and gnats, also deceived in this way, are important pollinators of many greenhoods.

Orchid names: The text of this book includes at least one common name for each species as well as a designated binomial name which consists of a genus name and species epithet. For example, the common name Brittle Greenhood is associated with the botanical name of *Diplodium truncatum, Diplodium* being the name of the genus and *truncatum* being the species name. Botanically, binomial names are more accurately applied than common names, which often arise from general usage or popularity. A species can have several common names but only a single accurate binomial name in any one classification. Unfortunately, parallel classification systems can be found in some groups of plants, orchids especially, and in this example, the applicable alternate binomial name to Brittle Greenhood is *Pterostylis truncata*. The common names used in this book are those that are widely adopted or commonly accepted.

Arrangement of the orchids: The native orchids included in this book are arranged alphabetically by their botanical names within their tribes (name ending in -eae such as Diurideae) or subtribes (name ending in -inae such as Drakaeinae) and these tribes and subtribes are arranged alphabetically throughout the text. The names of genera and species used in this book are based on the results of recent molecular-based genetic studies and may cause some confusion to readers as they will often differ from traditional concepts. For example, early workers treated all greenhoods in the genus *Pterostylis,* but modern treatments may recognise up to eight genera in this important group of native orchids. I have chosen to follow this modern classification because it is the way of the future and lines up with similar studies in the ferns, lilies and many other plant groups, however, it must be acknowledged that not all herbaria, botanists and orchid enthusiasts will accept these changes. Consequently, I have included names used in alternative systems of classification (AKA) in the text. In some cases, earlier names are also included (PKA), which will hopefully help to track nomenclatural name changes.

Abbreviations used in the text:

AKA	also known as
Aust.	Australia
c.	circa, approximately
Dec, Jan, Feb, etc	December, January, February, etc
E(e)	east
Indon.	Indonesia
Infl.	inflorescence
Is.	island(s)
N(n)	north
NCal	New Caledonia
NG	New Guinea
NSW	New South Wales
NT	Northern Territory
Occas.	occasionally
PKA	previously known as
Qld	Queensland
Ra.	ranges
S(s)	south
SA	South Australia
sp.	species singular
spp.	species plural
Tas	Tasmania
tlnds.	tablelands
Vic	Victoria
W(w)	west
WA	Western Australia

Alphabetical overview of genera included in this book

Acianthus (Acianthiinae): Terrestrial. 12 spp. endemic Aust. also NZ. Leaf single, heart-shaped. Racemes multiflowered. Flowers small, mosquito-like, green/pinkish. Labellum with 2 basal, tonsil-like, nectar-producing glands.

Adelopetalum (Bulbophyllinae): Epiphytic. 14 spp., 11 endemic Aust., others NZ, NCal. Clumping plants. Leaf 1 per pseudobulb. Racemes 1-flowered to multiflowered, from rhizome nodes. Flowers with thick fleshy unlobed labellum.

Anzybas (Acianthiinae): Terrestrial. 9 spp., 7 endemic Aust., 2 NZ. Leaf single, rounded. Flower single, tubular with apical opening subtended by beak-like structure. Labellum base with 2 open-ended auricles.

Arthrochilus (Drakaeinae): Terrestrial. 12 spp., most Aust., also NG. Dimorphic. Non-flowering plant a rosette. Flowering plants leafless, basal rosette developing later. Racemes multiflowered, lengthening as flowering proceeds. Sepals and petals recurved. Labellum hinged, swinging free, presented like an insectiform lure.

Australorchis (Grastidiinae): Epiphytic. 4 spp. endemic Aust. Clumping plants. Leaves 1–3 per pseudobulb. Racemes multiflowered, from upper axils. Sepals and petals similar. Labellum stiffly attached, 3-lobed.

Bunochilus (Pterostylidinae): Terrestrial. 30 spp. endemic Aust. Dimorphic. Non-flowering plants a rosette. Flowering plants a stem with spreading leaves and a multiflowered raceme of smallish, hooded flowers, deflexed lower lip and exposed 3-lobed labellum which, when triggered, shuts off entry to the flower.

Caladenia (Caladeniinae): Terrestrial. 300 spp., most endemic Aust., others NZ, NCal, East Timor, Indon. Most parts hairy. Leaf single. Flowers 1–6, from small and hand-like to large and spidery. Sepals and petals similar, often with terminal clubs (osmophores). Labellum hinged, stiffly or tremulous, margins often fringed with teeth, surface with rows of calli. NOTES: Important genus with many distinct groups.

Calanthe (Collabinae): Terrestrial. 150 spp., 1 Aust., others Africa to Asia. Evergreen or deciduous clumpers. Pseudobulbs short. Leaves 1 to several per pseudobulb, plicate, petiolate. Racemes axillary, multiflowered. Flowers crowded, white or colourful. Labellum stiffly attached, entire or deeply lobed, with basal spur.

Caleana (Drakaeinae): Terrestrial. Single endemic sp. Leaf single, basal. Flowers 1–5, resembling a flying duck. Sepals and petals recurved. Labellum resembling a duckbill, attached by an actively motile elastic claw. Column deeply basin-like.

Calochilus (Thelymitrinae): Terrestrial. 30 spp., most Aust., others NZ, NG, NCal. Leaf present or absent, single, much longer than wide. Racemes multiflowered. Flowers green/brown, segments often striate. Dorsal sepal broad, hooding column. Lateral sepals larger than petals. Labellum fixed, unlobed or obscurely 3-lobed, mostly covered with hairs (resembling a bushy beard).

Cestichis (Malaxideae): Epiphytic. 20 spp., 7 endemic Aust., others NG, Indon., Malaysia, Asia. Clumping plants. Pseudobulbs short. Leaves few per pseudobulb. Racemes multiflowered, arising with the new shoots. Flowers dull coloured, often smelly. Sepals and petals similar. Labellum stiffly attached, unlobed, sharply recurved near middle.

Chiloglottis (Drakaeinae): Terrestrial. 30 spp., most Aust., 4 extending to NZ. Leaves 2 in basally opposed pair. Flower single, either resembling an insect or young bird awaiting food. Sepals narrow, with small apical clubs. Petals spreading or recurved. Labellum either stiffly fixed or tremulous, adorned with calli, often insectiform.

Coelandria (Dendrobiinae): Epiphytic. Single sp. extending to Aust., others NG, Indon. Clumping plants. Pseudobulbs cane-like. Leaves several per pseudobulb, lasting 12 months. Racemes multiflowered, from apical nodes. Bird-pollinated flowers densely crowded, tubular. Labellum with contrasting shiny apex.

Corunastylis (Prasophyllinae): Terrestrial. 77 spp., most endemic Aust., 2 NZ, 1 NCal. Leaf single, cylindrical, solid, with short free apical blade. Leaf and flower stem inseparably fused together. Racemes terminal, short, multiflowered. Flowers small, glabrous or hairy. Dorsal sepal broad, hooding column. Sepals longer than petals. Labellum hinged, often tremulous, unlobed, glabrous or hairy.

Corybas (Acianthiinae): Terrestrial. 12 spp., 6 endemic Aust., others NZ, NG, NCal. Leaf single, ground-hugging. Flower single, helmet-like. Dorsal sepal greatly enlarged, enclosing most of the labellum. Labellum base with 2 closed spurs.

Corysanthes (Acianthiinae): Terrestrial. 20 spp. endemic Aust. Leaf single, ground-hugging. Flower single, helmet-like. Dorsal sepal and labellum enlarged. Labellum base tubular with 2 open auricles.

Cryptostylis (Cryptostylidinae): Terrestrial. 25 spp., 5 Aust., 1 NZ, others NG, Indon. Evergreen (1 sp. leafless), clumping. Leaves erect, petiolate. Racemes multiflowered. Flowers unusual shape, tepals narrow, inconspicuous. Labellum large, glandular hairy, marked with shiny ridges and rounded calli. NOTES: All 5 native spp. pollinated by Orchid Dupe Wasp (*Lissopimpla excelsa*) attracted by sexual deceit (see photo on page 9).

Cyanicula (Caladeniinae): Terrestrial. 10 spp. endemic WA. Most plant parts hairy. Leaf single. Flowers 1–4, mostly blue. Sepals and petals similar. Labellum hinged, unlobed (1 sp. 3-lobed), margins entire, surface with numerous small calli. NOTES: Flowers of several spp. close at night.

Cymbidium (Cymbidiae): Epiphytic. 50 spp., 3 endemic Aust., others NG, Indon., Asia. Clumping plants. Pseudobulbs or stems present. Leaves strap-like or channelled. Racemes multiflowered, axillary. Sepals and petals similar. Flowers often fragrant. Labellum hinged, 3-lobed.

Cyrtostylis (Acianthiinae): Terrestrial. 8 spp., 6 endemic Aust., 2 NZ. Leaf single, ground-hugging. Racemes multiflowered. Flowers small, insect-like, green/pinkish. Tepals narrow. Labellum broad, 2 conical basal nectaries.

Davejonesia (Grastidiinae): Epiphytic. 3 spp. endemic Aust. Rhizomes creeping. Pseudobulbs absent. Leaves alternate, thick, fleshy. Flowers single from rhizome near recently mature leaf.

Sepals broad, petals narrow. Labellum flexible, tongue-like, obscurely 3-lobed.

Dienia (Malaxideae): Terrestrial. 320 spp., 6 Aust., others NG, Polynesia, Asia. Deciduous clumpers with annually replaced above-ground fleshy stems. Leaves few, broad, plicate. Racemes terminal, multiflowered. Flowers tiny, crowded. Sepals broader than petals. Labellum 3-lobed, side lobes projecting back behind column.

Diplocaulobium (Grastidiinae): Epiphytic. 105 spp., 1 extending to Aust., others Indon., Polynesia, Asia. Clumping plants. Rhizomes creeping. Leaf 1 per pseudobulb. Flowers single, often in groups, produced sporadically, short-lived (hours). Sepals and petals similar. Labellum flexible, 3-lobed.

Diplodium (Pterostylidinae): Terrestrial. 80 spp., most endemic Aust., others NZ, NCal. Dimorphic. Non-flowering plants a rosette. Flowering plants a stem with sheathing/spreading leaves and 1–(2) hooded flowers, lower lip erect, closing off front of flower, labellum unlobed, mostly enclosed within flower. Distinct group has stem-encircling basal rosette.

Dipodium (Eulophinae): Terrestrial. 40 spp., 14 endemic Aust., others NG, Indon., NCal. Asia. Leaves present or absent. Racemes multiflowered. Flowers opening widely, colourful. Sepals and petals similar. Labellum stiffly hinged, projecting forwards, deeply 3-lobed, apical hair patch.

Diuris (Diuridinae): Terrestrial. 106 spp., most endemic Aust., 1 sp. Timor. Leaves basal, terete or channelled. Flowers distinctive, colourful. Sepals and petals dissimilar. Petals erect like ears. Dorsal sepal hooding column. Lateral sepals narrow, downcurved. Labellum fixed, deeply 3-lobed. NOTES: Important genus with many distinct groups.

Dockrillia (Grastidiinae): Epiphytic. 29 spp., 20 Aust., others NG, Indon., NCal., Polynesia. Clumping plants with erect/pendulous stems and terete leaves, or creeping rhizomes and appressed flattish leaves. Pseudobulbs absent. Racemes 1-flowered to few-flowered, from node near leaf base. Sepals usually broader than petals. Labellum flexible, 3-lobed.

Drakaea (Drakaeinae): Terrestrial. 10 spp. endemic WA. Leaf single, basal, spongy. Flower single, on tall thin stem, bizarre shape. Sepals and petals inconspicuous, recurved. Labellum with long basal foot, hinged, swinging free, remarkably insectiform, presented like a lure.

Durabaculum (Grastidiinae): Epiphytic. 76 spp., 13 Aust., others NG, Indon., NCal., Philippines, Polynesia. Clumping plants. Pseudobulbs short, swollen, or extended and cane-like. Leaves several per pseudobulb. Racemes multiflowered. Flowers long-lived. Petals larger than sepals. Labellum hinged, 3-lobed.

Elythranthera (Caladeniinae): Terrestrial. 2 spp. endemic WA. Most parts hairy. Leaf single. Flowers 1–4, small, glossy, enamel-like lustre. Sepals and petals similar. Labellum stiffly hinged, no calli, a basal pair of anther-like appendages.

Empusa (Malaxideae): Terrestrial. 7 spp., 1 extending to Aust., others NG, Indon., NCal, South America, Asia. Deciduous or evergreen clumpers. Pseudobulbs short, above ground. Leaves few, broad, plicate. Racemes terminal on new growth, multiflowered. Flowers small. Lateral sepals broader than dorsal sepal and petals. Labellum unlobed, sharply recurved near middle.

Epiblema (Thelymitrinae): Terrestrial. Single sp. endemic WA. Leaf single, terete, hollow. Racemes few-flowered. Flowers opening widely, not closing at night, bluish/mauve with dark veins and spots. Sepals and petals similar. Labellum unlobed, shortly stalked, flattish, two ribbon-like appendages at base.

Eriochilus (Caladeniinae): Terrestrial. 16 spp. endemic Aust. Leaf single, basal or attached above ground to flower stem. Flowers small, unusual shape. Lateral sepals enlarged, projecting downwards, white. Petals small, stalked. Labellum flexible, its base tubular, sharply recurved near middle, fleshy, with tufts of hairs.

Erythrorchis (Vanilliae): Terrestrial. 3 spp., 1 endemic Aust., others NG, Indon., Philippines, Asia. Deciduous leafless climbers with thick roots. Stems blackish, thin, wiry, supported by unbranched aerial roots. Panicles multiflowered. Flowers colourful, fragrant. Labellum flexible, lobed or unlobed.

Eulophia (Eulophinae): Terrestrial. 250 spp., 5 Aust., others Africa, Asia, Polynesia. Leafy deciduous clumpers (few leafless) with rhizomes, tubers or pseudobulbs. Leaves grass-like or plicate. Racemes multiflowered. Flowers colourful. Sepals and petals similar. Labellum stiffly attached, 3-lobed.

Gastrodia (Gastrodieae): Terrestrial. 20 spp., 6 Aust., others NZ, NG, Asia. Leafless orchids with rootless rhizomes. Racemes multiflowered on fleshy stem. Flowers tubular, dull-coloured, enclosing column and labellum. Sepals and petals fused together, petal tips free. Labellum flexible, 3-lobed.

Genoplesium (Prasophyllinae): Terrestrial. Single sp., endemic Aust. Leaf single, cylindrical, solid, with short free apical blade. Leaf and flower stem inseparably fused together. Raceme terminal, short, few-flowered. Flowers small, glabrous. Dorsal sepal hooding column. Lateral sepals much longer than petals. Labellum flexible, unlobed, glabrous.

Glossodia (Caladeniinae): Terrestrial. 2 spp. endemic Aust. Most parts hairy. Leaf single. Flowers 1–3, mauve/purple. Sepals and petals similar. Labellum stiffly hinged, no calli, basal pair of anther-like appendages.

Grastidium (Grastidiinae): Epiphytic. 500 spp., 5 Aust., others NG, Indon., NCal., Asia. Clumping plants. Pseudobulbs absent. Stems thin, flattish leafy. Flowers single or in pairs, from nodes opposite a leaf. Paired flowers face inwards towards each other. Flowers colourful, short-lived (1–2 days). Sepals and petals similar. Labellum hinged, 3-lobed.

Hymenochilus (Pterostylidinae): Terrestrial. 24 spp., most endemic Aust., others NZ. Monomorphic. Flowering plants have a stem-encircling basal rosette and multiflowered raceme of small, hooded flowers, pouched lower lip and exposed unlobed labellum which, when triggered, shuts off entry to the flower.

Kaurorchis (Bulbophyllinae): Epiphytic. 5 spp., 1 endemic Aust., others NG, NCal. Rhizomes creeping. Pseudobulbs tiny, each with a single fleshy leaf. Racemes multiflowered, from rhizome nodes. Flowers tiny, in dense terminal heads.

Leporella (Drakaeinae): Terrestrial. Single sp. endemic Aust. Leaf single or paired, broad. Flowers 1–3, unusual shape. Dorsal sepal hooding column. Lateral sepals deflexed. Petals club-shaped, covered with black glands, held erect like horns. Labellum weakly hinged, wider than long, fringed.

Leptoceras (Caladeniinae): Terrestrial. Single sp. endemic Aust. Leaf single, broad. Flower 1, unusual shape. Dorsal sepal hooding column. Lateral sepals projected obliquely downwards. Petals thin, glandular, held erect like horns. Labellum stiffly hinged, 2 rows of calli.

Lyperanthus (Megastylidinae): Terrestrial. 2 spp. endemic Aust. Leaf single, narrow, margins thickened. Racemes few-flowered. Flowers green/brown. Dorsal sepal broad, hooding column. Lateral sepals and petals narrow. Labellum flexible, 3-lobed, with crowded calli.

Microtidium (Prasophyllinae): Terrestrial. Single sp. endemic Aust. Leaf single, cylindrical, solid, with short free apical blade. Leaf and flower stem inseparably fused together. Raceme short, multiflowered. Flowers small, crowded, glabrous, green. Dorsal sepal broad, hooding column. Lateral sepals about as long as petals, both spreading. Labellum firmly fixed.

Microtis (Prasophyllinae): Terrestrial. 27 spp., most Aust., others NZ, Polynesia, Asia. Leaf single, cylindrical, hollow, with long free apical blade. Raceme/spike grows through leaf and emerges at weak point, multiflowered. Flowers small, crowded, glabrous, mostly green or white. Dorsal sepal broad, hooding column. Lateral sepals about as long as petals. Petals often partially enclosed in dorsal sepal. Labellum firmly fixed, unlobed.

Nervilia (Nerviliae): Terrestrial. 65 spp., 6 Aust., others NG, Indon., Polynesia. Dimorphic. Non-flowering plants are a single broad, upright or round-hugging leaf. Flowering plants a few-flowered, fleshy raceme, basal leaf developing later. Flowers erect or nodding. Sepals and petals similar, narrow. Labellum flexible, 3-lobed.

Oberonia (Malaxideae): Epiphytic. 300 spp., 8 Aust., others Africa, Asia, Polynesia. Clumping plants comprised of fan-like tufts of leaves. Pseudobulbs absent. Leaves laterally flattened, base overlapping. Racemes multiflowered. Flowers tiny, crowded, arranged spirally or in whorls. Sepals broader than petals. Labellum 3-lobed.

Oligochaetochilus (Pterostylidinae): Terrestrial. 80 spp. endemic Aust. Monomorphic. Flowering plants have a stem-encircling basal rosette and multiflowered raceme of hooded, green to red/brown flowers, deflexed lower lip often with tail-like free points and exposed unlobed insectiform labellum which, when triggered, shuts off entry to the flower.

Orthoceras (Diuridinae): Terrestrial. 3 spp., 1 Aust., 1 NZ, 1 NCal. Leaves basal, grass-like. Flowers 1–9, distinctive. Sepals and petals dissimilar. Dorsal sepal hooding column. Lateral sepals narrow, horn-like, erect/outcurved. Labellum fixed, 3-lobed.

Oxysepala (Bulbophyllinae): Epiphytic 25 spp., 8 endemic Aust., others NG, Indon., Asia. Creeping/pendulous rhizomes covered with papery bracts. Pseudobulbs small, each with a thick fleshy leaf. Racemes 1-flowered, arising at intervals from rhizome nodes. Flowers small, with fleshy tepals.

Paraprasophyllum (Prasophyllinae): Terrestrial. 150 spp., most endemic Aust., c.5 NZ. Similar to *Prasophyllum* but less robust, not reproducing via daughter tubers, growing singly or in tufts and with short broad ovaries held at a wide angle to the flower stem (long narrow ovaries closely appressed to the flower stem in *Prasophyllum*).

Pecteilis (Orchidinae): Terrestrial. 75 spp., 17 Aust., others NG, Asia, Polynesia. Leaves few, basal, stem-encircling. Racemes multiflowered. Flowers white, green or yellow. Dorsal sepal overlapping petals to form hood. Lateral sepals mostly recurved. Labellum deeply 3-lobed with basal spur, all lobes thin.

Peristeranthus (Vandeae): Epiphytic. Single sp. endemic Aust. Stems semi-pendulous, tip upcurved. Leaves large, semi-drooping, tips often twisted. Racemes long, pendulous, multiflowered. Flowers small, facing downwards, green with crimson markings, fragrant. Sepals and petals narrow, similar. Labellum hinged.

Phaius (Collabinae): Terrestrial. 20 spp., 3 Aust., others Africa to Asia. Evergreen clumpers with thick roots. Pseudobulbs short or elongated. Leaves 1 to several per pseudobulb, plicate, petiolate. Racemes axillary, multiflowered. Flowers large, colourful. Labellum stiffly attached, entire or lobed, with basal spur.

Phalaenopsis (Vandeae): Epiphytic. Single sp. endemic Aust. Stems semi-pendulous. Leaves broad, semi-drooping, fleshy, apex unequally notched. Racemes/panicles long, arching, sparsely branched, multiflowered. Flowers large, moth-like, mostly white. Petals larger than sepals. Labellum stiffly attached, 3-lobed; midlobe with two antenna-like appendages.

Pharochilum (Pterostylidinae): Terrestrial. Single sp. endemic Aust. Dimorphic. Non-flowering plants a rosette. Flowering plants a stem with short leaves and multiflowered terminal raceme of narrow, hooded, flowers, semi-deflexed lower lip and mostly exposed 3-lobed labellum which, when triggered, shuts off entry to the flower.

Pheladenia (Caladeniinae): Terrestrial. Single sp. endemic Aust. Most parts hairy. Leaf single. Flower 1, blue. Labellum stiffly hinged, flexible, 4–8 rows of dimorphic columnar calli.

Plectorrhiza (Vandeae): Epiphytic. 4 spp. endemic Aust. Stems semi-pendulous (single sp. upright). Leaves short, leathery, semi-drooping. Racemes short, thin, few-flowered. Flowers small, fragrant. Sepals and petals narrow, similar. Labellum fixed.

Plumatichilos (Pterostylidinae): Terrestrial. 25 spp., most endemic Aust., others NZ. Monomorphic. Flowering plants have an extended stem-encircling basal rosette and single, hooded flower with darker stripes and patterns, deflexed lower lip and exposed filiform labellum which has a basal beak, coarse spreading hairs and apical knob. When triggered the labellum shuts off lower entry to flower.

Praecoxanthus (Caladeniinae): Terrestrial. Single sp. endemic WA. Dimorphic. Non-flowering plant a single, prostrate, glabrous green leaf with white veins. Flowering plants leafless. Flower 1. Sepals and petals similar. Labellum stiffly hinged, 3-lobed, curved in semi-circle, 2 rows of calli.

Prasophyllum (Prasophyllinae): Terrestrial. 15 spp. endemic Aust. Leaf single, cylindrical, hollow with long free apical lamina. Raceme grows through leaf and emerges at a weak point, multiflowered. Racemes multiflowered. Flowers upside-down, crowded, colourful. Dorsal sepal broader than other segments. Sepals longer than petals, occas. fused to form synsepalum. Labellum fixed, unlobed, white or colourful, surface with large fleshy plate-like callus.

Pseudovanilla (Vanilliae): Terrestrial. 9 spp., 1 Aust., others NG, Indon., Philippines, Polynesia. Robust, deciduous, leafless climbers with thick roots. Stems high growing, thick, fleshy, green, supported by branched and unbranched aerial roots. Nodes with green, leaf-like bracts. Panicles multiflowered. Flowers colourful, fragrant. Labellum flexible, lobed or unlobed.

Pterostylis (Pterostylidinae): Terrestrial. 40 spp., most endemic Aust., others NZ, NG, New Britain, NCal. Monomorphic. Flowering plants have a stem-encircling basal rosette and single hooded flowers with erect lower lip and exposed or partly exposed, unlobed, hinged labellum.

Pyrorchis (Megastylidinae): Terrestrial. 2 spp. endemic Aust. Leaves 1–3, basal, ground-hugging. Racemes few-flowered. Flowers white/pink/red. Dorsal sepal broad, hooding column. Lateral sepals and petals narrow, spreading. Labellum flexible, 3-lobed, with small calli.

Rhizanthella (Prasophyllinae): Terrestrial. 5 spp. endemic Aust. Leafless subterranean orchids. Rhizomes thick, fleshy rootless, branching, turning upwards produce a multiflowered capitulum just below soil level. Flowers small, tubular, facing inwards, in spiral rows, outer flowers opening first.

Sarcochilus (Vandeae): Epiphytic or lithophytic. 22 spp., most endemic Aust., others NCal. Stems either sparsely branched and semi-pendulous with spreading leaves or freely branching from base with stiffly upright, leathery leaves. Racemes short to long, multiflowered. Flowers narrow to rounded, often colourful and fragrant. Sepals and petals similar. Labellum hinged.

Speculantha (Pterostylidinae): Terrestrial. 23 spp. endemic Aust. Dimorphic. Non-flowering plants a rosette. Flowering plants a stem with short leaves and multiflowered raceme of small, narrow, hooded flowers, erect lower lip and unlobed labellum held within flower.

Stamnorchis (Pterostylidinae): Terrestrial. Single sp. endemic Aust. Dimorphic. Non-flowering plants a rosette. Flowering plants a stem with spreading leaves and few-flowered raceme of unusual, open-topped, jug-like flowers, obliquely erect lower lip with sharply recurved tips and small labellum mostly or wholly hidden within flower.

Sullivania (Drakaeinae): Terrestrial. 15 spp., most endemic Aust., 1 sp. extends to NZ. Leaf single, basal. Flowers 1–10, resembling a perched bird with an extended beak. Sepals and petals inconspicuous. Labellum beak-like, attached by an actively motile elastic claw. Column deeply basin-like.

Taeniophyllum (Vandeae): Epiphytic. 170 spp., 13 Aust., others NG, Indon., Polynesia, Asia. Stems vestigial. Roots green, photosynthetic. Leaves absent. Racemes thin, lengthening and flowering spasmodically. Flowers small, tubular or opening widely, short-lasting (hours/few days). Sepals and petals similar, fused together or free. Labellum fixed.

Thelychiton (Grastidiinae): Epiphytic. 20 spp., most Aust., others Indon., NCal., Vanuatu, Fiji. Clumping plants. Pseudobulbs cylindrical, tapered or tetragonal. Leaves few, apical. Racemes multiflowered, from upper axils. Flowers long-lived. Sepals broader than petals. Labellum stiffly hinged, 3-lobed.

Thelymitra (Thelymitrinae): Terrestrial. 106 spp., most Aust., others NZ, NG, Indon., NCal., Philippines Leaf single, much longer than wide. Racemes multiflowered. Flowers opening with hot sun, closing at night. Tepals, including labellum, remarkably similar. Labellum unlobed and unadorned. Column shape, colour and peripheral features important (appendages, hoods, hair tufts, lobes, papillae).

Trachyrhizum (Grastidiinae): Epiphytic. 9 spp., 1 endemic Aust., others NG, Indon., Solomons. Clumping plants with creeping rhizome. Pseudobulbs narrow, cane-like, leafy. Racemes few-flowered, from nodes opposite a leaf. Flowers cupped, colourful. Sepals much wider than petals. Labellum hinged, 3-lobed.

Tropilis (Grastidiinae): Epiphytic. 10 spp., 7 endemic Aust., 3 NCal. Clumping plants. Pseudobulbs cylindrical. Leaves few, apical.

Racemes multiflowered, from upper axils. Flowers mostly white. Sepals and petals similar, narrow. Labellum hinged, 3-lobed.

Urochilus (Pterostylidinae): Terrestrial. 7 spp. endemic Aust. Dimorphic. Non-flowering plants a rosette. Flowering plants a stem with spreading leaves and multiflowered raceme of hooded red/brown or green flowers, a broad deflexed lower lip and exposed tailed labellum which, when triggered, shuts off entry to the flower.

Vanda (Vandeae): Epiphytic or lithophytic. 50 spp., single sp. extending to Aust., others NG, Philippines, Asia. Stems short or long, fibrous, sparsely branched. Leaves flat and strap-like or cylindrical and fleshy. Racemes short, few-flowered. Flowers large, rounded. Sepals and petals similar, narrowed to basal stalk. Labellum fixed, 3-lobed.

Zeuxine (Goodyeriinae): Terrestrial. 50 spp., 1 endemic Aust., others Africa, Asia, Polynesia. Leaves few, stem-encircling, thin-textured. Racemes multiflowered. Flowers small, glabrous or hairy. Dorsal sepal overlapping petals to form hood. Lateral sepals spreading. Labellum lobed, basal part pouched, apical part spreading.

Opposite: *Caladenia carnea* (L. Copeland).

THE ORCHIDS

MAYFLY ORCHID *Acianthus caudatus*

Although widely distributed and often locally common, the wispy flowers of this colonial orchid can be difficult to see in the gloom which it favours. A single heart-shaped leaf supports a fleshy stem and raceme of dark reddish/purple flowers with long thread-like tips. The flowers smell like a wet dog. FLOWERING: Apr–Oct.

SIZE/ID: Leaf flat on ground, 10–30 x 5–20mm, purple underside. Flowers c.40 x 4mm.

RANGE/HABITAT: Qld (se), NSW, Vic, Tas, SA. Coast, mountains. Forest/woodland, heath.

DARK MOSQUITO ORCHID *Acianthus exsertus* (left)

SMALL MOSQUITO ORCHID *Acianthus pusillus* (right)

Two similar spp. that flower Mar–Aug, both with a single heart-shaped leaf (purplish beneath) and a raceme of small insect-like flowers. Coast to ranges in forest and heath.

A. exsertus has larger, darker, widely spaced flowers 12–16mm long and blackish labellum (to 6 x 4mm). Qld, NSW, ACT, Vic.

A. pusillus has smaller, paler, closely spaced flowers 8–12mm long with a green/reddish labellum (to 4.5 x 3mm). Qld, NSW, ACT, Vic, Tas.

BANDED HELMET ORCHID *Anzybas fordhamii*

Small, cryptic orchid often difficult to find in the dense habitats it favours. Can be locally common and much easier to see in the first season after a fire. A small heart-shaped leaf supports a nodding, reddish/purple flower with a tubular dorsal sepal and prominent pale bands on the labellum. PKA *Corybas fordhamii*. FLOWERING: Jul–Nov.

SIZE/ID: Leaf flat on ground, 3–20 x 12–16mm, green both sides. Flower 1, c.12–14mm long.

RANGE/HABITAT: Qld (se), NSW, Vic, Tas, SA. Mainly coast/near-coastal. Dense heath, melaleuca and teatree swamps.

FAIRY LANTERNS *Corybas barbarae*

Colony-forming terrestrial with a heart-shaped leaf and single crystalline white or pinkish, lantern-like flower, which is dominated by a curved, hooded dorsal sepal that hides most of the hairy labellum. Two, short, closed spurs protrude from the labellum base. FLOWERING: May–Jul.

SIZE/ID: Leaf flat on ground, 20–30 x 20–30mm, purplish underside. Flower 1, 25–30 x 12–15mm.

RANGE/HABITAT: Qld, NSW (Windsor Tlnd to Sydney, LHI). Coast, ranges, tlnds. Forest/woodland.

FRINGED HELMET ORCHID *Corysanthes fimbriata*

Common colony-former with a single leaf and a small, helmet-like, purplish flower nestling in the base. The prominent labellum has a central translucent dome and a fringe of spreading teeth. FLOWERING: May–Jul. PKA *Corybas fimbriatus*.

SIZE/ID: Leaf flat on ground, 15–40 x 15–40mm, round, bright green. Flower 1, 25–40 x 25–30mm, translucent with dark red/purple mottles.

RANGE/HABITAT: Qld (n to Atherton Tlnd), NSW, ACT, Vic, Tas. Coast, ranges. Forest/woodland, heath, scrub.

SMALL GNAT ORCHID *Cyrtostylis reniformis* (left)

LARGE GNAT ORCHID *Cyrtostylis robusta* (right)

Two commonly confused orchids. Both flower winter/spring, have a single, rounded, basal ground-hugging leaf and 1–8 insect-like flowers with a distinctive, flat, projecting labellum. Coast, ranges, inland. Forest, heath, mallee, under shrubs.

C. reniformis has blue/green leaf with distinctly paler veins and pink/purple labellum c.12 x 5mm. Qld (s), NSW, ACT, Vic, Tas, SA.

C. robusta has yellow/green to green leaf with indistinct veins and brownish labellum c.15 x 6mm. Vic (w), Tas (n, Bass Strait Is.), SA, WA.

PINEAPPLE ORCHID *Adelopetalum elisae*

Distinctive epiphyte recognised by its compact patches of crowded, pineapple-like pseudobulbs and greenish/yellow flowers (occas. pinkish/brownish) with unusually long lateral sepals. Mainly found well inland from the coast and distributed from se Qld to Blue Mtns of NSW. Grows on rocks, cliff faces and trees, often in fairly exposed sites. FLOWERING: May–Nov. PKA *Bulbophyllum elisae.*

SIZE/ID: Pseudobulbs 10–30 x 15–20mm. Leaves 60–100 x 8–12mm. Flowers 15–20 x 10–15mm.

TINY STRAND ORCHID *Adelopetalum exiguum*

Common epiphyte that ranges from se Qld to se NSW and forms spreading patches on rocks and cliffs, less commonly trees, in shady humid areas in wetter forests and gullies. Widely spaced, small, globose pseudobulbs are connected by a thin rhizome and the small cream to yellowish flowers are carried on thin, thread-like racemes. FLOWERING: Feb–Jun. PKA *Bulbophyllum exiguum*.

SIZE/ID: Pseudobulbs 5–10 x 6–8mm. Leaves 20–50 x 6–9mm. Flowers 5–6 x 8–10mm.

BLOTCHED WAX ORCHID *Adelopetalum weinthalii*

The young growths of this localised epiphyte are covered with soft white cottony sheaths. These break down as the growths mature and green pseudobulbs become prominent. Grows exclusively among mosses and lichens on the upper branches of large Hoop Pines in the mountains of se Qld and ne NSW. FLOWERING: Mar–May. PKA *Bulbophyllum weinthalii*.

SIZE/ID: Pseudobulbs 10–20 x 9–14mm. Leaves 20–30 x 5–9mm. Flowers smelly, 5–7 x 15–20mm, whitish with red and purplish spots/blotches, labellum purplish.

CREEPING BRITTLE ORCHID *Kaurorchis evasa*

Specialised orchid with creeping brittle stems, small widely spaced pseudobulbs each bearing a broad fleshy leaf, and tiny flowers in a dense recurved cluster atop a long thin flower-stem that widens near the apex. Grows on mossy boulders and trees in high altitude rainforest. Pink/reddish flowers have conspicuous dark red stripes and yellowish tips. FLOWERING: Nov–Mar. PKA *Bulbophyllum evasum.*

SIZE/ID: Pseudobulbs 2–3 x 4mm. Leaves 20–40 x 6–8mm. Flowers 4–5 x 2–3mm.

RED ROPE ORCHID *Oxysepala schilleriana*

Epiphyte with dangling stems supported from near the base by thin roots. Groups of brilliant orange/red flowers contrast with the fleshy, broadly grooved, dark green leaves, sometimes completely hiding the stems. From Mt Finnigan in ne Qld to near Newcastle in central NSW. Commonest in montane wet forests. FLOWERING: Apr–Aug. PKA *Bulbophyllum schillerianum*, *B. aurantiacum*.

SIZE/ID: Pseudobulbs 5–8 x 3–4mm. Leaves 30–100 x 15–25mm. Flowers 4–7 x 2–3mm.

WHEAT-LEAF ORCHID *Oxysepala shepherdii*

Ranging from near Nambour in se Qld to near Bega in se NSW, this common, clumping orchid grows on trees and rocks in rainforest and sheltered humid gullies with the rhizomes and broadly grooved leaves appressed close to the host. Small white/cream flowers have yellowish tips and an orange to red/brown labellum. FLOWERING: Mar–Oct. PKA *Bulbophyllum shepherdii*.

SIZE/ID: Pseudobulbs 2–3 x 4mm. Leaves 20–40 x 6–8mm. Flowers 4–5 x 2–3mm.

THREAD-TIPPED ROPE ORCHID *Oxysepala windsorensis*

Localised epiphyte restricted to the mountains and tlnds of ne Qld, growing on the upper branches of rainforest trees on ridgetops where there is abundant air movement and moisture. Stems dangling, attached by basal roots and covered by brown bracts. Cream/greenish flowers grouped along the stems have long thread-like tips. FLOWERING: May–Aug. PKA *Bulbophyllum windsorense*.

SIZE/ID: Pseudobulbs 5–8 x 4–5mm. Leaves 15–30 x 4–6mm. Flowers 10–15 x 12–15mm.

MOUNTAIN CAPS *Caladenia alpina*

Sturdy orchid of higher montane, subalpine and alpine regions, growing among grass and shrubs in moist loamy soil. A broad, fleshy leaf supports a thick, reddish scape and the white, musk-scented flowers have a broad hooding dorsal sepal and prominent red bands on the labellum. FLOWERING: Nov–Feb.

SIZE/ID: Leaf 1, 120–220 x 8–15mm. Scape 150–300mm long. Flowers 1–4, 30–35 x 30–35mm.

RANGE/HABITAT: NSW, ACT, Vic, Tas. Woodland, herbfields, streambanks, bogs.

DAINTY BLUE CALADENIA *Caladenia amplexans*

Commonest in drier areas well inland from the coast, this elegant orchid can be recognised by its pale blue flowers and the incurved labellum margins which clasp the column. Often grows in crowded colonies. FLOWERING: Aug–Oct. PKA *Cyanicula amplexans*.

SIZE/ID: Leaf 1, 60–125 x 5–7mm, prostrate, sparsely hairy. Scape 120–200mm long. Flowers 1–3, 15–20 x 18–22mm.

RANGE/HABITAT: WA (Nerren Nerren Station to Norseman). Woodland, shrubland, granite outcrops.

REACHING SPIDER ORCHID *Caladenia arrecta*

Easily recognised by its stiffly spreading red sepals and petals with relatively long, thick, furrowed, flattish, yellow/brown clubs, the petals upcurved as if reaching for the sky. The red labellum has a fringe of thin spreading teeth and four or six rows of dark red hockey-stick shaped calli. FLOWERING: Jul–Oct.

SIZE/ID: Leaf 1, 100–300 x 15–25mm. Scape 120–350mm long. Flowers 1–3, 30–50mm across.

RANGE/HABITAT: WA (Bindoon to Israelite Bay). Coast, inland. Forest/woodland, shrubland.

COMMON DRAGON ORCHID *Caladenia barbarossa*

Distinctive orchid with unusually shaped cream to greenish-yellow flowers with red markings. Narrow tepals spread outwards and the strongly curved, hairy labellum, which bears a remarkable resemblance to a wingless female flower wasp, is presented on a fleshy stalk extending from the column base. FLOWERING: Sep–Nov.

SIZE/ID: Leaf 1, 40–60 x 5–10mm. Scape 100–300mm long. Flowers 1–2, 20–40 x 20–30mm.

RANGE/HABITAT: WA (Bindoon to Esperance). Forest/woodland, swamp margins, granite outcrops.

BLUE CALADENIA *Caladenia caerulea*

One of the first orchids to flower in spring and frequently common in extensive patches. Recognised by the blue flowers (rarely white) and the blue labellum with darker blue transverse bars and pale-yellow/white tip. FLOWERING: Jul–Sep. PKA *Cyanicula caerulea*.

SIZE/ID: Leaf 1, 30–60 x 3–5mm, prostrate. Scape 80–150mm long. Flower 1, 20–30 x 20–30mm.

RANGE/HABITAT: Qld (n to Blackdown Tlnd), NSW, ACT, Vic. Coast, mountains, inland. Forest, rock outcrops.

ZEBRA ORCHID *Caladenia cairnsiana*

The conspicuous whitish to creamy/yellow, smooth-margined, upswept labellum of this orchid is boldly striped like a zebra and adorned with a short central band of crowded, blackish calli. By contrast the inconspicuous narrow sepals and petals are held closely against the ovary. FLOWERING: Aug–Nov.

SIZE/ID: Leaf 1, 50–200 x 4–6mm. Scape 120–300mm long. Flowers 1–2, 10–15mm across.

RANGE/HABITAT: WA (Lancelin to Esperance). Mallee, heath, forest.

PINK FINGERS *Caladenia carnea* (left)

DUSKY FINGERS *Caladenia fuscata* (right)

Two commonly confused orchids flowering Aug–Nov with a narrow hairy leaf and similar white or pink flowers with red bars on the labellum. Both occur in Qld, NSW, ACT, Vic, Tas, SA in forest, heath, mallee.

C. carnea flowers later and has 1–5 larger, more brightly coloured flowers with straight, upright labellum lobes.

C. fuscata flowers 2–3 weeks earlier than *C. carnea*, always with a single, smaller flower with dusky external bands and incurved labellum lobes.

WHITE FINGERS *Caladenia catenata* (left)

PAINTED FINGERS *Caladenia picta* (right)

Two very similar common orchids. Both have a single narrow hairy leaf and similar white or pink flowers with an orange tip on the labellum. Both grow in coastal heath, shrubland and forest/woodland and flower profusely in wet years.

C. catenata flowers spring (Aug–Oct) and has a green column. Qld, NSW, Vic (e).

C. picta flowers autumn/winter (Apr–Jun) and has a wholly red or patchy red column. Qld, NSW (Gladstone to Eden).

CHAPMAN'S SPIDER ORCHID *Caladenia chapmanii*

Clumping spider orchid with red or cream/yellow flowers with drooping/pendulous lateral sepals and petals that end in thin wispy glandular tails which tangle readily. The broad creamy white labellum has prominent red stripes, short marginal teeth and two rows of flattish anvil-shaped calli. FLOWERING: Sep–Oct.

SIZE/ID: Leaf 1, 150–200 x 2–5mm. Scape 200–450mm long. Flowers 1–4, 100–120mm across.

RANGE/HABITAT: WA (Yallingup to Waroona, Boyup Brook to Northam, disjunct near Kulin). Forest/woodland, shrubland.

DANCING SPIDER ORCHID *Caladenia discoidea*

Common orchid of the south-west with distinctive flowers that dance in the wind. The squat yellow/pink flowers can be recognised by spreading petals and wide, deeply fringed, red-veined labellum with a central band of crowded blackish calli. FLOWERING: Apr–Oct.

SIZE/ID: Flowers. Leaf 1, 80–200 x 5–10mm. Scape 100–400mm long. Flowers 1–4, 25–40mm across.

RANGE/HABITAT: WA (Kalbarri to Israelite Bay, inland to Hyden). Mallee, heath, forest/woodland, salt-lake margins.

FRINGED MANTIS ORCHID *Caladenia falcata*

Widespread, common orchid with reclining green/yellow spidery flowers heavily marked with red. The lateral sepals, downcurved at first then strongly upswept, end in thin light brown clubs. The delicately hinged labellum, green with a maroon apex and long marginal comb-teeth, trembles in the lightest breeze. FLOWERING: Aug–Oct.

SIZE/ID: Leaf 1, 100–200 x 5–15mm. Scape 200–400mm long. Flower 1–3, 50–80mm across.

RANGE/HABITAT: WA (Wongan Hills to Jerramungup). Mallee, woodland, granite outcrops.

COWSLIP ORCHID *Caladenia flava* subsp. *flava*

Conspicuous with its pale yellow to bright yellow flowers (often marked with red), this widespread common orchid often grows in extensive crowded colonies. Found in sandy/gravelly soils in forested and shrubby habitats. Flowers well in unburnt habitats but enhanced by summer fires. FLOWERING: Jul–Dec.

SIZE/ID: Leaf 1, 60–150 x 10–15mm. Scape 100–250mm long. Flowers 1–4, 20–40 x 20–40mm.

RANGE/HABITAT: WA (Kalbarri to Israelite Bay). Coast, inland. Forest/woodland, shrubland, rock outcrops.

FUNNEL-WEB SPIDER ORCHID *Caladenia infundibularis*

Late-flowering sp. recognised by green and yellow flowers with a large projecting yellow labellum with a red apex, the base sunken like a funnel, the margins with a fringe of numerous, thin, spreading comb teeth and the surface with rows of relatively small reddish calli. FLOWERING: Oct–Dec.

SIZE/ID: Leaf 1, 100–260 x 8–14mm. Scape 250–450mm long. Flowers Oct–Dec, 1–3, 60–80mm across.

RANGE/HABITAT: WA (Dunsborough to Northcliffe). Coastal scrub, forest/woodland.

PINK FAIRIES *Caladenia latifolia*

Widely distributed in southern areas from the coast to well inland. A large prostrate leaf supports a thick, hairy scape and the pink flowers (rarely white) have long marginal teeth on the labellum. Grows in colonies often with a low proportion of flowering plants. FLOWERING: Aug–Dec.

SIZE/ID: Leaf 1, 80–180 x 15–25mm. Scape 100–450mm long. Flowers 1–4, 25–30 x 25–30mm.

RANGE/HABITAT: Vic, Tas, SA, WA. Coastal scrub, forest, rock outcrops, limestone.

LARGE WHITE SPIDER ORCHID *Caladenia longicauda*

Common spider orchid with large creamy white flowers, erect dorsal sepal and spreading/pendulous lateral sepals and petals with long yellowish filamentous tips. The broad creamy/white labellum has a fringe of thin white-tipped teeth and four rows of hockey-stick shaped calli, FLOWERING: Oct–Dec.

SIZE/ID: Leaf 1, 180–250 x 5–15mm. Scape 350–600mm long. Flowers Sep–Oct, 1–4, 60–110mm across.

RANGE/HABITAT: WA (New Norcia to Albany). Coast, adjacent inland. Forest/woodland.

MUSKY CAPS *Caladenia moschata*

The flowers of this musk-scented orchid are white internally, the outer surfaces ranging from green/brown to red/brown or purplish from a dense covering of tiny glands. The column is hooded by an incurved cap-like dorsal sepal and the white labellum is often marked with purple. FLOWERING: Oct–Dec.

SIZE/ID: Leaf 1, 100–220 x 4–8mm. Scape 150–300mm long. Flowers 1–5, 16–20 x 25–32mm.

RANGE/HABITAT: NSW, ACT, Vic, SA (se). Coast, mountains. Forest, often drier forests.

LAZY SPIDER ORCHID *Caladenia multiclavia*

Amazing orchid in which the red-striped/-stained greenish/yellow flower resembles a reclining spider resting on its back. The filamentous upper halves of the tepals sweep upwards around the incredible diamond-shaped labellum which is boldly marked with red stripes and has a dense central mass of calli resembling a resting insect. **FLOWERING:** Sep–Oct.

SIZE/ID: Leaf 1, 40–100 x 5–10mm. Scape 100–250mm long. Flowers 1–2, 30–40mm across.

RANGE/HABITAT: WA (Borden to Ravensthorpe). Forest/woodland, shrubland.

DROOPING SPIDER ORCHID *Caladenia radialis*

Often found growing in clumps, this attractive orchid can be recognised by the eye-catching labellum boldly adorned with red stripes and subtended by spreading cream tepals with densely glandular, strongly drooping red tips. Two bands of short cream to red slender calli line the centre of the labellum. FLOWERING: Aug–Oct.

SIZE/ID: Leaf 1, 50–80 x 5–7mm. Scape 150–350mm long. Flowers 1–2, 40–80mm across.

RANGE/HABITAT: WA (Northampton to Jerramungup). Forest/woodland, shrubland, rock outcrops.

KOPPIO SPIDER ORCHID *Caladenia septuosa*

Of restricted distribution but often locally common, this handsome orchid grows among rocks and shrubs on sheltered slopes. Its green and reddish flowers have thick yellow/brown clubs and the almost triangular, maroon-tipped labellum (base green) has long comb-teeth and rows of tall red/maroon calli. FLOWERING: Sep–Oct.

SIZE/ID: Leaf 1, 60–80 x 7–10mm. Scape 150–250mm long. Flower 1, 25–35mm across.

RANGE/HABITAT: SA (Eyre Pen.). Mallee, sparse woodland, shrubland.

EASTERN MANTIS ORCHID *Caladenia tentaculata*

Recognised by its large green, white and red/maroon flowers which appear to be reclining – an impression created by the long lateral sepals that project forwards in front of the labellum, upcurved near the base and with droopy brownish tips. FLOWERING: Sep–Dec.

SIZE/ID: Leaf 1, 80–150 x 12–20mm. Scape 150–500mm long. Flowers 1–3, 60–100mm across.

RANGE/HABITAT: NSW, Vic, SA. Higher rainfall coast to lower ranges. Heathy forest, grassy forest/woodland.

THICK-LIP SPIDER ORCHID *Caladenia tessellata*

Relatively widespread but generally uncommon, this species is characterised by the yellowish/reddish flowers and the large heart-shaped labellum with its crowded rows of black calli. The lateral sepals and petals decurve towards the hairy ovary soon after the flowers open. FLOWERING: Sep–Oct.

SIZE/ID: Leaf 1, 50–100 x 4–9mm. Scape 80–150mm long. Flowers 1–3, 10–30mm across.

RANGE/HABITAT: NSW, Vic (Swansea to Wonthaggi). Coastal scrub, heathy forest, open forest.

BLUE CHINA ORCHID *Cyanicula gemmata*

Widespread western orchid that flowers profusely in areas burnt the previous summer. The blue/mauve/purple flowers with their widely spreading segments open widely on warm/hot days, close loosely at night and remain closed in cool weather. Leaf reddish beneath. FLOWERING: Aug–Nov. AKA *Caladenia gemmata*.

SIZE/ID: Leaf 1, 25–40 x 15–20mm. Scape 50–150mm tall. Flowers 1–3, 30–50 x 30–50mm.

RANGE/HABITAT: WA (Kalbarri to Israelite Bay). Coast, inland. Forest/woodland, shrubland, heath.

SILKY BLUE ORCHID *Cyanicula gemmata*

Stately orchid with a relatively broad, silky-hairy leaf and lovely mauve/blue flowers with spreading/arching tepals. The three-lobed labellum has lateral lobes closely clasping the column, small recurved midlobe and the exterior marked with dark blue spots. FLOWERING: Aug–Nov. AKA *Caladenia sericea*.

SIZE/ID: Leaf 1, 60–120 x 15–25mm. Scape 150–400mm tall. Flowers Aug-Nov, 1–4, 35–50 x 35–50mm.

RANGE/HABITAT: WA (Jurien Bay to Esperance). Coast, adjacent inland. Tall wetter forest, coastal scrub, rock outcrops.

PURPLE ENAMEL ORCHID *Elythranthera brunonis* (left)

PINK ENAMEL ORCHID *Elythranthera emarginata* (right)

Two similar common WA orchids with hairy leaf, colourful glossy flowers and unusual labellum appendages. Both grow in woodland/forest, shrubland, heath.

E. brunonis Flowers spring (Aug–Oct), 1–3, to 30 x 30mm, purple, pinker with age. Labellum tip upcurved; appendages purple with yellow base. WA (Kalbarri to Israelite Bay).

E. emarginata Flowers spring/summer (Oct–Dec), 1–4, to 45 x 45mm, bright pink. Labellum tip whitish, folded in tight S-bend; appendages dark purple, swollen. WA (Jurien Bay to Ravensthorpe).

EASTERN BUNNY ORCHID *Eriochilus cucullatus*

Summer-/autumn-flowering orchid with flowers that have prominent projecting white lateral sepals, tightly incurved dorsal sepal hooding the column, narrow, white-tipped petals spreading like arms and a strongly curved labellum furnished with tufts of red or white bristles. FLOWERING: Jan–Apr.

SIZE/ID: Leaf 1, 15–35 x 7–12mm. Scape 100–250mm long. Flowers 1–5, 15–20 x 12–15mm.

RANGE/HABITAT: Qld, NSW, ACT, Vic, Tas, SA (se). Coast, mountains, inland plains. Forest, grassland, heath.

COMMON BUNNY ORCHID *Eriochilus multiflorus*

Tall, multiflowered sp. with an obliquely erect leaf on the flower stem well above ground level, and small green and red flowers with contrasting white lateral sepals. The leaf increases in size as flowering progresses. Flowers best after fire. FLOWERING: Mar–Jun. AKA *Eriochilus dilatatus* subsp. *multiflorus*.

SIZE/ID: Leaf 1, 15–45 x 5–15mm. Scape 200–450mm long. Flowers 1–20, 10–15 x 10–12mm.

RANGE/HABITAT: WA (Perth to Albany). Forest/woodland.

PINK BUNNY ORCHID *Eriochilus scaber* subsp. *scaber*

Winter-/spring-flowering orchid with dimorphic leaves. Non-flowering plants have dark green leaves with white veins, whereas flowering plants have pale green cupped leaves at the base of a thickish flower stem. Flowers pink/white with a red labellum, best after fire. FLOWERING: Jun–Sep.

SIZE/ID: Leaf 1, 8–20 x 5–15mm. Scape 20–50mm long. Flowers 1–3, 8–11 x 9–12mm.

RANGE/HABITAT: WA (Jurien Bay to Israelite Bay). Winter/wet areas, rock outcrops.

WAXLIP ORCHID *Glossodia major* (left)

SMALL WAXLIP ORCHID *Glossodia minor* (right)

Two similar common orchids with single hairy leaf, colourful flowers and unusual labellum appendages. Both in woodland/forest, shrubland, heath.

G. major scape to 300mm tall. Flowers spring (Aug–Nov), 1–3, to 45 x 45mm, mauve/purple. Labellum appendage yellow. Qld, NSW, ACT, Vic, Tas, SA. Coast, mountains, inland plains. AKA *Caladenia major.*

G. minor scape to 150mm tall. Flowers winter/spring (Jul–Oct), 1–2, to 25 x 25mm, purple. Labellum appendage purple, base yellow. Qld, NSW, Vic (e). Mainly coastal. AKA *Caladenia glossodia.*

RABBIT ORCHID *Leptoceras menziesii*

Interesting orchid with unusually shaped white/pinkish flowers, the lateral sepals spreading in front of the red-barred labellum and the red petals erect like a pair of ears. Extensive dense colonies. Flowers profusely after summer fires. FLOWERING: Aug–Nov.

SIZE/ID: Leaf 1, 40–90 x 15–30mm. Scape 80–250mm long. Flowers 1–3, 15–20 x 10–15mm. Labellum 5.5–7 x 5.5–7mm.

RANGE/HABITAT: Vic, Tas, SA, WA. Coast, inland. Mallee, heathy forest, heath.

BLUEBEARD ORCHID *Pheladenia deformis*

Distinctive orchid that grows singly or in crowded tufts. Can be recognised by its bright blue sweetly scented flowers (occas. pinkish, white or yellow) and two types of column-like calli that form a crowded mass on the labellum. FLOWERING: Jun–Oct. AKA *Caladenia deformis*.

SIZE/ID: Leaf 1, 40–100 x 3–5mm. Scape 50–150mm tall. Flower 1, 25–35 x 30–40mm.

RANGE/HABITAT: NSW, Vic, Tas, SA, WA. Coast, inland plains. Forest, mallee, heath, rock outcrops.

RAINBOW ORCHID *Praecoxanthus aphyllus*

Autumn-flowering gem with colourful, yellowish, highly fragrant flowers which have a prominent purple, green and yellow labellum with rows of yellow-tipped calli. A single flower is carried atop a tall thin leafless stem. The green-and-white leaf arises on a separate plant. FLOWERING: Mar–May.

SIZE/ID: Leaf 1, 8–18 x 6–8mm. Scape 200–450mm long. Flower 1, 25–35 x 25–35mm. Labellum 8–13 x 6–8mm.

RANGE/HABITAT: WA (Pinjarra to Albany, Esperance). Forest, scrub, heath.

CHRISTMAS ORCHID *Calanthe australasica*

Evergreen orchid with large, dark green, pleated leaves and conspicuous tall racemes of white flowers. Labellum divided into 4 lobes with conspicuous yellow basal callus. Grows among litter in shady locations, often on rotting logs and stumps. FLOWERING: Oct–Feb.

SIZE/ID: Pseudobulbs 40–80 x 20–40mm. Leaves 4–9, 40–900 x 100–180mm. Scape 500–1,500mm long. Flowers many, 30–40 x 25–35mm.

RANGE/HABITAT: Qld, NSW (Iron Ra. to Termeil). Wetter forests.

SWAMP ORCHID *Phaius tankervilleae*

Evergreen orchid with large, pale green, pleated leaves and conspicuous tall racemes of large colourful flowers, reddish-brown internally, externally white (and in in bud). Labellum with prominent basal spur. FLOWERING: Sep–Nov.

SIZE/ID: Pseudobulbs 50–70 x 50–70mm. Leaves 4–7, 500–1,250 x 80–100mm. Scape 500–2,000mm long. Flowers 4–16, 60–100 x 65–110mm.

RANGE/HABITAT: Qld, NSW (Laura to Kempsey); also NG, Asia. Swamps, springs, seepage sites. Moist/wet soil.

BONNET ORCHID *Cryptostylis erecta*

Popular orchid valued for its intriguing flowers that have a large, erect, concave, bonnet-like labellum that is beautifully marked with purple lines and patterns. Leaves upright, green above, red/purple beneath. FLOWERING: Jun–Mar.

SIZE/ID: Scape 300–800mm tall. Leaves 1–4 in clusters, 80–180 x 25–30mm. Flowers 2–12, 25–30 x 10–15mm.

RANGE/HABITAT: Qld, NSW, ACT, Vic (e). Coast, mountains. Forest/woodland, heath, grassy flats.

SLIPPER ORCHID *Cryptostylis ovata*

Recognised by distinctive dark green leaves with a contrasting white midrib and purple/red underside, the flowers of this common western orchid have a projecting, yellowish, hairy labellum marked with a network of dark red veins. FLOWERING: Oct–Apr.

SIZE/ID: Scape 250–700mm tall. Leaves 1–6 in clusters, 190–250 x 40–80mm, dark green above with white midrib, purple beneath. Flowers 4–15, 20–30 x 15–20mm.

RANGE/HABITAT: WA (Perth to Mt Ragged). Forest/woodland, heath, shrubland, swamp margins, rock outcrops.

LARGE TONGUE ORCHID *Cryptostylis subulata*

The flowers of this widespread, common orchid are dominated by a stiffly decurved, glandular hairy labellum which is green and red/brown/purple with strongly recurved margins and two dark ridges ending in a bilobed knob. FLOWERING: Aug–Apr.

SIZE/ID: Scape 500–800mm tall. Leaves 1–6 in clusters, 80–150 x 25–30mm, green both sides. Flowers 3–20, 25–35 x 10–14mm.

RANGE/HABITAT: Qld, NSW, ACT, Vic, Tas, SA; also NZ. Coast, mountains. Forest/woodland, heath, swamps.

CHANNEL-LEAF CYMBIDIUM *Cymbidium canaliculatum*

This large epiphyte projects from tree hollows as coarse clumps of large crowded pseudobulbs and deeply channelled grey/green leaves. Long arching racemes carry fragrant flowers in an array of colours and patterns. FLOWERING: Sep–Oct.

SIZE/ID: Pseudobulbs 80–120 x 30–40mm. Leaves 2–6, 300–500 x 30–40mm. Racemes 200–400mm long. Flowers 5–90, 25–45 x 20–40mm.

RANGE/HABITAT: WA (n), NT (n), Qld, NSW (Cape York to Ardlethan). Coast, ranges, inland slopes. Drier forests.

NATIVE CYMBIDIUM *Cymbidium madidum*

Commonly found on trees with thick papery or fibrous bark, this epiphyte can grow into very large clumps. Swollen crowded pseudobulbs carry erect/arching flat green leaves and pendulous racemes of scented green/brown flowers. FLOWERING: Aug–Dec.

SIZE/ID: Pseudobulbs 120–250 x 40–60mm. Leaves 4–8, 300–900 x 30–40mm. Racemes 200–600mm long. Flowers 10–70, 22–35 x 20–30mm.

RANGE/HABITAT: Qld, NSW (Cape York to Port Macquarie). Coast, adjacent ranges. Wetter forests, paperbark swamps.

SWEET CYMBIDIUM, SNAKE ORCHID *Cymbidium suave*

Recognised by its narrow, fibre-covered stems (no pseudobulbs), this epiphyte projects from tree hollows as a grassy clump with narrow strap-shaped leaves and willowy stems. Long racemes carry numerous green/yellow sweetly scented flowers. FLOWERING: Aug–Jan.

SIZE/ID: Stems 300–500 x 15–20mm. Leaves 4–8, 300–450 x 15–20mm. Racemes 100–300mm long. Flowers 5–50, 22–35 x 20–30mm.

RANGE/HABITAT: Qld, NSW (Cape York to Bournda). Coast, adjacent ranges. Humid forest/woodland.

BOTTLEBRUSH ORCHID *Ceraia smillieae*

Distinctive epiphyte with crowded spindle-shaped, knobbly pseudobulbs with dark rings on the nodes, thin-textured leaves which fall after a year and pink/white semi-tubular flowers densely packed in bottlebrush-like spikes. FLOWERING: Aug–Nov. PKA *Dendrobium smillieae.*

SIZE/ID: Pseudobulbs 300–1,000 x 20–30mm. Leaves 13–21, 150–200 x 30–40mm. Racemes 80–150mm long. Flowers numerous, 15–25 x 10–18mm.

RANGE/HABITAT: Qld (Torres Strait to Townsville). Coast, mountains. Wetter forests, mangroves, swamps.

WHITE DOUBLETAIL *Diuris alba*

The lightly scented flowers of this elegant orchid are mainly white, lightly marked with red or lilac/mauve. The petals splay outwards in a characteristic manner and the labellum midlobe is flat with small upcurved side lobes. Two narrow tail-like lateral sepals hang beneath the labellum. FLOWERING: Jul–Sep.

SIZE/ID: Leaves 1–3, 100–300 x 2–3mm. Scape 150–400mm tall. Flowers 2–7, 20–25mm across.

RANGE/HABITAT: Qld, NSW (Sarina to Wyong). Coast, adjacent ranges. Heath, wallum, grassy forest.

GIANT DONKEY ORCHID *Diuris amplissima*

Tall, large-flowered donkey orchid with yellow/brown to brown flowers stained with purple suffusions. The deeply 3-lobed labellum has a purple midlobe with downcurved margins and spreading yellow/brown sidelobes. The broad dorsal sepal is upright behind the labellum and the narrow lateral sepals hang downwards. FLOWERING: Sep–Nov.

SIZE/ID: Leaves 2–3, 100–220 x 2–2.5mm. Scape 400–900mm tall. Flowers 3–8, 30–50mm across.

RANGE/HABITAT: WA (Darken to Mount Barker). Inland. Grassy/shrubby areas, forest/woodland.

GOLDEN DONKEY ORCHID *Diuris aurea*

Handsome orchid with large golden/orange flowers lightly marked with brown. The large paddle-shaped petals project upwards like ears and the jutting labellum has a large central lobe folded down the middle with two broad spreading side lobes. **FLOWERING:** Aug–Nov.

SIZE/ID: Leaves 2, 100–250 x 4–8mm. Scape 300–600mm tall. Flowers 2–5, 30–35mm across.

RANGE/HABITAT: NSW (Kurri Kurri to Ulladulla). Coast, ranges. Grassy forest, heath, heathy forest.

WESTERN WHEATBELT DONKEY ORCHID

Diuris brachyscapa

Early spring-flowering donkey orchid that grows in colonies and produces colourful floral displays. Plants have relatively short flower stems and pale-yellow flowers with red to red/brown markings, mainly on the labellum which has a short downcurved midlobe and spreading narrow side lobes. FLOWERING: Jul–Sep.

SIZE/ID: Leaves 2–3, 120–250 x 8–12mm. Scape 150–400mm tall. Flowers 1–4, 20–30mm across.

RANGE/HABITAT: WA (Wongan Hills to Ravensthorpe). Wheatbelt. Grassy/shrubby forest, rock outcrops.

GOLDEN MOTHS *Diuris chryseopsis*

This orchid has an upright tuft of narrow grassy leaves and pale yellow flowers with a few dark small marks and internal streaks. The flowers are wider than long with spreading petals and a large flat labellum with small, toothed side lobes. FLOWERING: Aug–Oct.

SIZE/ID: Leaves 4–9, 50–150 x 2–4mm. Scape 100–300mm tall. Flowers 1–4, 17–30mm across.

RANGE/HABITAT: NSW (n to Orange), ACT, Vic, Tas. Coast, ranges. Grassy forest, grassland, shrubby forest.

LATE MAUVE DOUBLETAIL *Diuris dendrobioides*

Widespread orchid which can be recognised by its widely spaced, lightly scented flowers with long thin lateral sepals dangling/projecting downwards like tails and whitish, lilac to mauve flowers marked with darker purple spots, speckles and striae. FLOWERING: Nov–Jan.

SIZE/ID: Leaves 1–2, 100–250 x 3–7mm. Scape 200–400mm tall. Flowers 1–9, 25–35mm across.

RANGE/HABITAT: NSW (n to Deepwater), ACT, Vic (ne). Inland ranges, plains. *Callitris* forest, grassy forest, grassland.

YELLOW GRANITE DONKEY ORCHID *Diuris hazeliae*

Prominent orchid of inland granite outcrops and drainage lines. Grows in crowded colonies and produces eye-catching colourful displays of bright yellow flowers with some brown markings on the labellum. The large petals diverge like ears and the labellum lobes are relatively narrow, the short midlobe with downturned margins. FLOWERING: Aug–Sep.

SIZE/ID: Leaves 2–4, 100–300 x 4–7mm. Scape 150–400mm tall. Flowers 1–6, 25–35mm across.

RANGE/HABITAT: WA (Paynes Find to Balladonia). Inland. Shallow gravelly soil.

PURPLE PANSY ORCHID *Diuris longifolia*

Striking, but variable orchid with colourful flowers in shades of mauve, purple, pink and brown, overlaid with yellowish suffusions. The broad paddle-shaped petals spread upwards like ears and the labellum has a short, strongly folded midlobe and two larger, widely spreading side lobes. Flowers best after fire. FLOWERING: Sep–Dec.

SIZE/ID: Leaves 2–3, 100–250 x 8–10mm. Scape 100–350mm tall. Flowers 2–8, 20–30mm across.

RANGE/HABITAT: WA (Perth to Albany). Coast, adjacent inland. Wetter forests, shrubland.

DONKEY ORCHID *Diuris orientis*

Widespread locally common orchid with yellow flowers variably suffused with pale red to red/brown or mauve shades and darker colours in the labellum midlobe, occas. wholly yellow flowers with no markings. Often seen on burnt ground in crowded clonal colonies with all flowers in the colony remarkably uniform. FLOWERING: Sep–Nov.

SIZE/ID: Leaves 1–3, 100–300 x 5–10mm. Scape 100–400mm tall. Flowers 1–6, 30–50mm across.

RANGE/HABITAT: NSW (se), Vic, Tas, SA. Coast, adjacent inland. Heathy forest, heath.

PURPLE DOUBLETAIL *Diuris punctata*

Spectacular ground orchid with large mauve to purple flowers with a prominent yellow patch on the labellum which has a large midlobe and relatively small spreading side lobes. Two long tail-like lateral sepals hang beneath the labellum. Historically recorded in extensive colonies. FLOWERING: Sep–Dec.

SIZE/ID: Leaves 2, 100–300 x 5–6mm. Scape 300–600mm tall. Flowers 1–10, 50–60mm across.

RANGE/HABITAT: NSW (n to Moonbi), ACT, Vic. Coast, ranges, inland plains. Grassy forest, grassland.

TIGER ORCHID, HORNET ORCHID *Diuris sulphurea*

Widespread, often common orchid recognised by its bright yellow flowers with darker markings, especially two dark brown/blackish blotches prominent on the base of the dorsal sepal. Grows in clonal colonies and flowers best after fire. FLOWERING: Aug–Nov.

SIZE/ID: Leaves 1–3, 100–500 x 3–4mm. Scape 200–500mm tall. Flowers 1–7, 20–30mm across.

RANGE/HABITAT: Qld, NSW, ACT, Vic, Tas, SA (se). Coast, mountains, inland plains. Forest/woodland, shrubland, heath.

GOAT ORCHID *Diuris tricolor*

Distinctive orchid of the inland, mostly growing among tussocks and scattered shrubs in sparse forests. Plants are relatively tall with yellow to orange flowers centrally marked with red, purple and white speckles and long decurved green/brown lateral sepals. Single plant known from Vic. FLOWERING: Sep–Nov.

SIZE/ID: Leaves 1–3, 200–300 x 3–4mm. Scape 200–500mm tall. Flowers 2–6, 25–30mm across.

RANGE/HABITAT: Qld (s), NSW, Vic (ne). Inland slopes, plains. *Callitris* forest, drier forests.

HORNED ORCHID *Orthoceras strictum*

Distinctive orchid recognisable by its basal tuft of grassy leaves, stiffly erect habit and long narrow lateral sepals that spread out widely from each flower like a pair of horns. Flower colour includes brown, black or green, all with a prominent yellow patch on the labellum. FLOWERING: Oct–Jan.

SIZE/ID: Plants 300–600mm tall. Leaves 2–5, 150–300 x 2–3mm. Flowers 1–9, 8–10mm across.

RANGE/HABITAT: Qld, NSW, ACT, Vic, Tas, SA. Coast, mountains, inland slopes. Forest/woodland, heath, swamps.

WISPY ELBOW ORCHID *Arthrochilus prolixus*

Racemes carrying small bluish/green flowers arise before the rosettes of leaves appear. The flowers, in which the lateral sepals and petals reflex back against the ovary, have a projecting curved column and a hinged reddish insect-like labellum. FLOWERING: Dec–Feb.

SIZE/ID: Scape 120–320mm tall. Leaves 2–6, 40–70 x 7–15mm. Flowers 3–22, 10–16mm long. Labellum c.5 x 0.6mm.

RANGE/HABITAT: Qld, NSW (Gympie to Mona Vale). Coast, ranges. Forest/woodland, coastal scrub.

FLYING DUCK ORCHID *Caleana major*

Popular orchid with flowers that have a remarkable resemblance to a flying duck. Its labellum, which is shaped like a duck's head and beak, snaps shut when triggered by a visiting insect or inquisitive child. FLOWERING: Sep–Feb.

SIZE/ID: Scape 200–500mm tall. Leaf 1, 80–120 x 6–8mm, spongy, green/pink with darker streaks and spots. Flowers 1–5, 20–25 x 6–7mm. Labellum 6.5–8 x 5–6mm.

RANGE/HABITAT: Qld, NSW, Vic, Tas, SA. Coast, mountains. Forest/woodland, shrubland, heath.

DUCK'S HEAD ORCHID *Chiloglottis anaticeps*

Distinctive orchid which has bright green to brownish flowers, sepals with long thin clubs, petals reflexed against the ovary and a horizontal labellum, the surface covered with massed calli and the main gland shaped remarkably like the head of a duck. FLOWERING: Aug–Nov.

SIZE/ID: Scape 35–70mm tall. Leaves 2, 30–40 x 14–18mm. Flower 1, 26–30 x 5–6mm. Labellum 9–11 x 5–6mm.

RANGE/HABITAT: NSW (Northern Tlnds). Mountains, Tlnds. Wetter forests, streambanks.

DIAMOND ANT ORCHID *Chiloglottis trapeziformis*

Widespread common orchid that grows in crowded patches. The green to brownish flowers are held stiffly erect with the diamond-shaped labellum adorned with a small group of blackish calli resembling the head of an ant. FLOWERING: Aug–Nov.

SIZE/ID: Scape 80–120mm tall. Leaves 2, 50–80 x 15–25mm. Flower 1, 12–16 x 6–8mm. Labellum 8–12 x 6–8mm.

RANGE/HABITAT: Qld, NSW, ACT, Vic, Tas, SA (se); also NZ. Coast, mountains, inland slopes. Forest/woodland, heath.

LARGE BIRD ORCHID *Chiloglottis valida*

The flowers of this common bird orchid are greenish/brown to purplish/brown and its broad, heart-shaped labellum is so delicately attached at the base that it can tremble in a breeze and shut when tripped by a pollinator. FLOWERING: Sep–Jan.

SIZE/ID: Scape 40–70mm tall. Leaves 2, 50–100 x 20–40mm. Flower 1, 20–30 x 30–35mm. Labellum 14–18.5 x 12–16mm.

RANGE/HABITAT: NSW, ACT, Vic; also NZ. Coast, mountains. Wetter forests, streambanks, swamp margins, sphagnum bogs.

KING-IN-HIS-CARRIAGE *Drakaea glyptodon*

Intriguing orchid best identified by the dark red/purple, insect-like labellum which has a plump swollen body covered with bristly hairs, short straight hairless tail and narrow neck covered with shiny black warts. Strong floral scent on warm/hot days. FLOWERING: Aug–Oct.

SIZE/ID: Scape 100–350mm tall. Leaf 1, 20–30mm across, prostrate, spongy, heart-shaped, blue/grey with darker veins and margins. Flower 1. Labellum 6–8 x 3–4mm.

RANGE/HABITAT: WA (Enneaba to e of Esperance). Coast, inland. Forest/woodland, shrubland, heath in moist sand.

WARTY HAMMER ORCHID *Drakaea livida*

Identified by the dark red/purple, insect-like labellum with a pale green central section, dark purple warts and hairs, a knobbly head covered with shiny black warts and hairs, a hairless tail arising at right angles and strongly spotted labellum stalk. FLOWERING: Aug–Oct.

SIZE/ID: Scape 100–350mm tall. Leaf 15–20mm across, prostrate, spongy, heart-shaped, blue/grey with network of darker veins. Flower 1. Labellum 10–12 x 3.5–4mm.

RANGE/HABITAT: WA (Watheroo to Ravensthorpe). Forest/woodland, shrubland, heath in sand.

FRINGED HARE ORCHID *Leporella fimbriata*

The pale-coloured flowers of this orchid, carried on a thin, wiry stem, have two upright ear-like petals and a broad hinged labellum with delicately fringed margins. Single or paired leaves are bluish/green with red veins. Large, sparse colonies. Flowers best after fire. FLOWERING: Mar–Jun.

SIZE/ID: Scape 100–300mm tall. Leaves 1–2, 15–55 x 5–25mm. Flowers 1–3, 20–25 x 7–10mm. Labellum 4–5 x 8–10mm.

RANGE/HABITAT: Vic, SA, WA. Coast, inland. Forest/woodland, coastal scrub, heath.

SMALL DUCK ORCHID *Sullivania minor*

Similar in general appearance to the Flying Duck Orchid but with much smaller greener flowers and a narrower labellum covered with shiny black calli. Flowers best after summer fires. **FLOWERING:** Oct–Mar. AKA *Caleana minor*.

SIZE/ID: Scape 50–150mm tall. Leaf 1, 50–120 x 1–2mm, often withered at flowering. Flowers 1–7, 8–11 x 5–7mm. Labellum 5–5.5 x 3.5–4mm.

RANGE/HABITAT: Qld, NSW, ACT, Vic, Tas, SA; also NZ. Coast, mountains, inland. Forest/woodland, heath, shrubland.

DRUMMOND'S DUCK ORCHID *Sullivania nigrita*

Common sp. that can be recognised by its ovate turgid leaf, its underside dark red, and the green to reddish flower with a longish, narrow labellum humped in the middle (obvious from side). FLOWERING: Aug–Oct. AKA *Paracaleana nigrita, Caleana nigrita.*

SIZE/ID: Scape 50–150mm tall. Leaf 1, 15–30 x 7–11mm. Flowers 1–(2), 15–25 x 7–10mm. Labellum 10–14 x 3–4mm.

RANGE/HABITAT: WA (Eneabba to Israelite Bay). Forest/woodland, shrubland, heath, granite outcrops.

BLOTCHED HYACINTH ORCHID *Dipodium punctatum* (left)

ROSY HYACINTH ORCHID *Dipodium roseum* (right)

Two leafless summer-flowering orchids which have dark, fleshy stems and showy colourful flowers with narrow spreading tepals and protruding hairy labellum. Coast to hills and mountains in heath and forest.

D. punctatum has pink flowers heavily marked with dark pink spots/blotches and flat tepals (tips not recurved). Qld, NSW, ACT, Vic, Tas, SA.

D. roseum has pale/rose-pink flowers with small dark pink spots and tepals with recurved tips. Qld, NSW, ACT, Vic, Tas, SA (se).

SHEPHERD'S CROOK ORCHID *Eulophia picta*

Terrestrial orchid with large crowded pseudobulbs, each with a conspicuous group of pleated leaves and a cluster of pink or white bell-shaped flowers on the end of a curved flower stem. FLOWERING: Dec–Feb. PKA *Geodorum densiflorum, G. pictum.*

SIZE/ID: Pseudobulbs to 50 x 30mm. Leaves 3–5, to 350 x 80mm. Scape 200–300mm tall. Flowers 8–20, c.24 x 20mm.

RANGE/HABITAT: WA (n), NT (n), Qld, NSW (Torres Strait to Kempsey). Coast, mountains, tlnds. Wetter forests, heath, grassland.

TALL POTATO ORCHID *Gastrodia procera* (left)

COMMON POTATO ORCHID *Gastrodia sesamoides* (right)

Leafless orchids with fleshy brown stems and fragrant bell-shaped flowers, externally brownish, white internally. Labellum tip just visible.

G. procera: Flowering Dec–Jan. Stems 500–1,200mm tall, 10–75 flowers. Racemes straight in bud. NSW, ACT, Vic, Tas, SA (se). Mainly higher montane forest.

G. sesamoides: Flowering Sep–Jan. Stems 120–500mm tall, 4–25 flowers. Racemes nodding in bud. Qld, NSW, ACT, Vic, Tas, SA (se). Coast, mountains. Forest/woodland, coastal scrub.

JEWEL ORCHID *Zeuxine oblonga*

Common in Qld but generally uncommon/rare elsewhere, this shade-loving orchid has a basal group of dark green net-veined leaves, hairy flower stem and terminal spike of small, pale green/pinkish flowers with prominent 2-lobed white/cream labellum. FLOWERING: Jul–Oct.

SIZE/ID: Leaves 3–7, to 80 x 30mm. Scape 100–300mm tall. Flowers 5–40, c. 4 x 3mm.

RANGE/HABITAT: WA (n), NT (n), Qld, NSW (Torres Strait to Bellingen). Coast, mountains, tlnds. Rainforest, swamp margins, track margins.

LILY-OF-THE-VALLEY ORCHID *Australorchis monophylla*

Distinctive epiphyte with slender conical pseudobulbs, narrow dark green leaves and upright racemes of sweetly scented, yellow, waxy, bell-shaped flowers. Often grows in strong light. FLOWERING: Aug–Dec. AKA *Dendrobium monophylum.*

SIZE/ID: Pseudobulbs 60–120 x 20–30mm. Leaves 1–2, 80–120 x 25–30mm. Racemes 100–150mm long. Flowers 5–20, 5–7 x 6–8mm.

RANGE/HABITAT: Qld, NSW (Cooktown to Grafton). Coast, mountains, tlnds. Humid forest.

PILLAR ORCHID *Davejonesia prenticei*

Often locally common, this epiphyte can be recognised by its characteristic, dark green, straight or curved, fleshy, pillar-shaped leaves. Small, red-striped flowers with orange/yellow labellum arise singly on a thin stalk. Trunks and outer branches of trees. FLOWERING: sporadically. AKA *Dendrobium prenticei.*

SIZE/ID: Stems creeping. Leaves 25–40 x 4mm. Flowers single, 4–5 x 5–7mm.

RANGE/HABITAT: Qld (Mt Finnigan to Mt Spec). Coast, mountains, tlnds. Mangroves, rainforest, relict paddock trees.

CREEPING STAR ORCHID *Diplocaulobium glabrum*

Locally common epiphyte that forms crowded clumps of shiny yellowish/green pseudobulbs each topped with a single leathery leaf. Short-lived (8–10 hours), spidery flowers, white with pale yellow tips, arise at intervals, especially during the wet season. FLOWERING: sporadically.

SIZE/ID: Pseudobulbs 40–50 x 12–15mm. Leaf 1, 60–75 x 10–15mm. Flowers 20–25 x 20–25mm.

RANGE/HABITAT: Qld (Torres Strait to Cairns); also NG. Coast, mountains. Humid forest.

STRAGGLY PENCIL ORCHID *Dockrillia bowmanii*

Straggly epiphyte on trees and rocks. Sparsely branched, semi-pendulous stems support small dark green cylindrical leaves. Small groups of yellowish/green flowers, each with a conspicuous white labellum, appear in flushes. FLOWERING: Aug–Jun. AKA *Dendrobium bowmanii.*

SIZE/ID: Stems to 600mm long. Leaves 50–150 x 4mm. Racemes 10–20mm long. Flowers 1–4, 16–22 x 20–25mm.

RANGE/HABITAT: Qld, NSW (Forty Mile Scrub to Woodburn); also NCal. Coast, ranges, inland. Mangroves, swamps, dry rainforest, gorges.

TABLELAND PENCIL ORCHID *Dockrillia calamiformis*

Showy clusters of white flowers contrast with pendulous, dark green cylindrical leaves of this large, dangling clumping epiphyte. Trees and rocks in higher ranges and tlnds, often on ridges where clouds and mists are frequent. FLOWERING: Aug–Nov. AKA *Dendrobium calamiforme*.

SIZE/ID: Stems to 1m long. Leaves 100–250 x 2–3mm. Racemes 50–80mm long. Flowers 3–5, 30–38 x 25–35mm.

RANGE/HABITAT: Qld (Windsor Tlnd to Paluma Ra.). Ranges, tlnds. Rainforest, street trees, park trees.

CUCUMBER ORCHID, GHERKIN ORCHID

Dockrillia cucumerina

Identified by its small, bumpy, gherkin-like leaves and tight groups of attractive cream/yellowish flowers with red stripes, this orchid spreads on rocks and trees on humid slopes and streambanks. Commonest inland from the coast. FLOWERING: Nov–Mar. AKA *Dendrobium cucumerinum*.

SIZE/ID: Stems creeping. Leaves 20–35 x 5–12mm. Racemes 30–50mm long. Flowers 2–6, 9–12 x 12–20mm.

RANGE/HABITAT: Qld, NSW (Bunya Mtns to Picton). Coast, ranges, inland slopes. Open forest, streambanks.

THUMBNAIL ORCHID, TICK ORCHID *Dockrillia linguiformis*

Common epiphyte with fleshy, dark green, tongue-like leaves closely appressed to the host. Racemes of white flowers with narrow, pointed segments produce an attractive display. Forms spreading patches on rocks, boulders and trees, often in bright light. FLOWERING: Jun–Sep. AKA *Dendrobium linguiforme*.

SIZE/ID: Stems creeping. Leaves 20–40 x 12–15mm. Racemes 60–150mm long. Flowers 6–20, 7–9 x 8–13mm.

RANGE/HABITAT: Qld, NSW (Gympie to Bega). Coast, ranges, inland slopes. Forest/woodland, rainforest, gorges.

DAGGER ORCHID *Dockrillia pugioniformis*

Hard dark green to yellowish leaves with a sharp rigid point are a useful feature to identify this epiphyte which grows in tangled masses and dangling strands on rocks and trees. Greenish flowers with a purple-spotted white labellum arise singly at the leaf bases. FLOWERING: Sep–Nov. AKA *Dendrobium pugioniforme*.

SIZE/ID: Stems dangling. Leaves 30–70 x 15–20mm. Flowers single, 10–15 x 15–20mm.

RANGE/HABITAT: Qld, NSW (Bunya Mtns to Wyndham). Coast, mountains. Shady humid forest.

STREAKED ROCK ORCHID *Dockrillia striolata*

Dense clumping lithophyte forming extensive patches on boulders and cliffs. Short thick terete leaves, often curved, take on reddish tones in bright light. Yellowish flowers with red/brown external stripes and white labella, project out from the clumps. FLOWERING: Sep–Nov. AKA *Dendrobium striolatum.*

SIZE/ID: Stems to 600mm long. Leaves 40–120 x 3–4mm. Racemes 10–30mm long. Flowers 1–2, 12–16 x 15–20mm.

RANGE/HABITAT: NSW (s), Vic (e), Tas (Bass Strait Is.). Coast, ranges. Forest, streambanks, gorges.

BRIDAL VEIL ORCHID *Dockrillia teretifolia*

Showy clusters of fragrant white flowers on the dangling clumps of this widespread epiphyte contrast with pendulous, dark green cylindrical leaves. Often prominent on sheoaks in coastal swamps. FLOWERING: Jul–Aug. AKA *Dendrobium teretifolium.*

SIZE/ID: Stems to 2m long. Leaves 300–600 x 4–6mm. Racemes 50–100mm long. Flowers 3–15, 20–30 x 30–40mm.

RANGE/HABITAT: Qld, NSW (Calliope to Narooma). Coast, ranges. Mangroves, swamps, rainforest, humid open forest.

MAUVE BUTTERFLY ORCHID *Durabaculum bigibbum*

Very similar in growth habit and floral features to the Cooktown Orchid (*D. phalaenopsis*) but occurring much further north and with a distinctive white patch of papillae on the labellum. FLOWERING: Feb–Jul. AKA *Dendrobium bigibbum*.

SIZE/ID: Pseudobulbs 200–1,200 x 10–15mm. Leaves 3–5, 100–150 x 30–35mm. Racemes 200–400mm long. Flowers 2–20, 20–30 x 30–60mm.

RANGE/HABITAT: Qld (Torres Strait to Archer R., Weipa). Coastal scrub, streambanks, humid thickets, gullies.

GOLDEN ORCHID *Durabaculum brownii*

Preferring exposed sunny locations, this robust, locally common epiphyte grows into large, untidy, tangled clumps. Long-lasting flowers in long racemes are variable in size, colour and floral patterns. FLOWERING: Aug–Nov. AKA *Dendrobium brownii*, *D. discolor*.

SIZE/ID: Pseudobulbs 1,000–5,000 x 40–60mm. Leaves 10–35, 80–160 x 35–50mm. Racemes 200–600mm long. Flowers 10–40, 40–80 x 40–80mm.

RANGE/HABITAT: Qld (Cape York to Seventeen Seventy). Coast, mountains. Coastal scrub, headlands, mangroves, humid forest.

WHITE BUTTERFLY ORCHID *Durabaculum dicuphum*

Epiphyte from northern tropical areas that grows rapidly in the wet season, the plants becoming dormant in the dry and usually shedding some, or all, of their leaves before flowering. FLOWERING: May–Aug. AKA *Dendrobium dicuphum*.

SIZE/ID: Pseudobulbs 150–700 x 15–25mm. Leaves 2–10, 80–200 x 20–30mm. Racemes 150–500mm long. Flowers 2–20, 25–30 x 25–50mm.

RANGE/HABITAT: Tropical NT, WA. Inland from coast. Rainforest thickets, paperbark swamps, gorges.

BLUE ANTELOPE ORCHID *Durabaculum nindii*

Renowned for its arching spikes of long-lasting, whitish/mauve flowers with contrasting violet/purple veins on the broad labellum, this specialised epiphyte grows in hot, humid conditions. FLOWERING: Jul–Sep. AKA *Dendrobium nindii.*

SIZE/ID: Pseudobulbs 500–2,500 x 30–40mm. Leaves 6–22, 80–150 x 40–80mm. Racemes 200–500mm long. Flowers Jul–Sep, 8–35, 50–60 x 50–60mm.

RANGE/HABITAT: Qld (Iron Ra. to Innisfail); also NG. Mainly coastal. Swamps, mangroves, rainforest.

COOKTOWN ORCHID *Durabaculum phalaenopsis*

Plants of this epiphyte, the floral emblem of Qld, have narrow conical pseudobulbs which produce racemes of large butterfly-like lilac/mauve flowers in the dry season when they are often leafless. FLOWERING: Mar–Jul. AKA *Dendrobium phalaenopsis.*

SIZE/ID: Pseudobulbs 200–1,200 x 10–15mm. Leaves 3–5, 100–150 x 30–35mm. Racemes 200–400mm long. Flowers 2–20, 25–50 x 25–80mm.

RANGE/HABITAT: Qld (Cooktown to Font Hills). Coastal scrub, rainforest thickets.

TEATREE ORCHID *Durabaculum tattonianum*

Commonly found on stunted paperbarks in swampy areas, this epiphyte has crowded onion-like pseudobulbs and thick, fleshy, deeply channelled leaves. Long arching racemes carry white flowers with twisted yellow tips. FLOWERING: Jul–Sep. AKA *Dendrobium tattonianum*.

SIZE/ID: Pseudobulbs 30–120 x 15–25mm. Leaves 2–6, 80–200 x 4–8mm. Racemes 100–300mm long. Flowers 5–50, 15–20 x 22–30mm.

RANGE/HABITAT: Qld (Laura to Rockhampton). Coast, ranges. Paperbark woodland, mangroves, swamps.

BLOTCHED GEMINI ORCHID *Grastidium baileyi*

Epiphytic orchid with thin, leafy, flattish, willowy stems that continue growth for two or three seasons and carry pairs of short-lived, spidery flowers in flushes throughout the year. FLOWERING: Sporadically. AKA *Dendrobium baileyi.*

SIZE/ID: Stems 300–1,200 x 3mm. Leaves numerous, dark green, 60–90 x 8mm. Flowers 20–30 x 20–30mm, yellow/green heavily spotted/blotched with red/purple, lasting only a few hours.

RANGE/HABITAT: Qld (McIlwraith Ra. to Bowen). Coast, mountains. Rainforest, mangroves, swamps.

SLENDER CANE ORCHID *Thelychiton adae*

Locally common tree/rock orchid that forms crowded clumps of thin pseudobulbs, each topped with dark green leathery leaves. Short racemes of widely opening, sweetly scented flowers, white, yellow or apricot coloured, appear in spring. FLOWERING: Jul–Oct. AKA *Dendrobium adae*.

SIZE/ID: Pseudobulbs 200–600 x 6mm. Leaves 2–4, 40–80 x 15–25mm. Racemes 10–40mm long. Flowers Jul–Oct, 1–8, 20–35 x 20–30mm.

RANGE/HABITAT: Qld (Cooktown to Paluma). Ranges, tlnds. Rainforest.

BEECH ORCHID *Thelychiton falcorostrus*

Epiphyte, mainly found on the upper trunks and larger branches of Antarctic Beech (*Nothofagus moorei*). Forms dense clumps of yellowish pseudobulbs with dark green leaves and produces contrasting clusters of strong-smelling white flowers. FLOWERING: Aug–Oct. AKA *Dendrobium falcorostrum.*

SIZE/ID: Pseudobulbs 200–500 x 10–15mm. Leaves 2–5, 80–150 x 20–30mm. Racemes 80–160mm long. Flowers 4–20, 32–38 x 30–35mm.

RANGE/HABITAT: Qld, NSW (McPherson Ra. to Barrington Tops). Mountains. Highland rainforest.

APRICOT CANE ORCHID *Thelychiton fleckeri*

Localised orchid growing on mossy trees, shrubs and rocks on ridgetops at high altitudes in the mountains and tlnds. Recognised by very thin pseudobulbs and relatively large, yellow to orange flowers with a protruding hairy labellum. FLOWERING: Oct–Dec. AKA *Dendrobium fleckeri*.

SIZE/ID: Pseudobulbs 150–300 x 3–5mm. Leaves 2–3, 50–80 x 20–25mm. Racemes 10–25mm long. Flowers 1–4, 27–30 x 25–30mm.

RANGE/HABITAT: Qld (Mt Finnigan to Ravenshoe). Mountains, tlnds. Rainforest.

BLOTCHED CANE ORCHID *Thelychiton gracilicaulis*

Common epiphyte that sometimes grows into large clumps. Plants have upright to semi-pendulous, slender pseudobulbs, dark green leaves and clusters of pleasantly fragrant yellow flowers heavily marked externally with red/brown blotches. FLOWERING: Jul–Sep. AKA *Dendrobium gracilicaule*.

SIZE/ID: Pseudobulbs 400–600 x 4–7mm. Leaves 3–7, 70–130 x 20–40mm. Racemes 50–100mm long. Flowers 5–30, 10–13 x 10–13mm.

RANGE/HABITAT: Qld, NSW (Monto to Gosford). Coast, mountains. Wetter forests.

PINK ROCK ORCHID *Thelychiton kingianus*

Boulders, cliff faces and gorges are the favoured habitats of this widespread clumping lithophyte. Crowded tapering pseudobulbs have grey/green leaves and relatively short racemes of pink/mauve flowers. New growths are often pink. FLOWERING: Apr–Nov. AKA *Dendrobium kingianum*.

SIZE/ID: Pseudobulbs 50–500 x 10–25mm. Leaves 2–7, 50–120 x 15–30mm. Racemes 80–200mm long. Flowers 1–15, 8–12 x 15–20mm.

RANGE/HABITAT: Qld, NSW (Biggenden to Newcastle). Coast, mountains.

ROCK ORCHID *Thelychiton speciosus*

Common clumping epiphyte usually growing on cliffs and boulders, less commonly trees. Plants have tough leathery pseudobulbs, large leathery leaves and long racemes of crowded, strongly scented, white/yellow flowers. FLOWERING: Jul–Oct. AKA *Dendrobium speciosum.*

SIZE/ID: Pseudobulbs 100–400 x 30–60mm. Leaves 2–5, 100–250 x 40–80mm. Racemes 200–600mm long. Flowers 30–100, 45–65 x 40–52mm.

RANGE/HABITAT: Qld, NSW, Vic (Yeppoon to Cann R.). Coast, ranges. Forest, gorges, boulders, rock outcrops.

TREE SPIDER ORCHID *Thelychiton tetragonus*

Unusual epiphyte with distinctive, 4-sided, pendulous pseudobulbs, each with a very thin base and dark green leaves. Starry, green/yellow and red flowers with relatively long narrow tepals arise on short racemes among the leaves. FLOWERING: May–Oct. AKA *Dendrobium tetragonum*.

SIZE/ID: Pseudobulbs 150–450 x 6–9mm. Leaves 2–5, 50–80 x 20–25mm. Racemes 10–35mm long. Flowers 1–5, 30–45 x 20–40mm.

RANGE/HABITAT: Qld, NSW (Fraser Is. to Nowra). Coast, mountains. Wetter forests, often near water.

BUTTERCUP ORCHID *Trachyrhizum agrostophyllum*

Locally common epiphyte with thin leafy pseudobulbs widely spaced on a creeping rhizome. Semi-drooping, bright yellow, waxy, sweetly scented flowers arise in small clusters from the upper nodes. **FLOWERING**: Jul–Nov. AKA *Dendrobium agrostophyllum.*

SIZE/ID: Pseudobulbs 100–600 x 5–10mm. Leaves 8–20, 40–100 x 8–12mm. Flowers 2–5, 10–15 x 15–20mm.

RANGE/HABITAT: Qld (near Cooktown to Paluma Ra.). Mountains, tlnds. Rainforest, humid slopes, swamps.

IRONBARK ORCHID *Tropilis aemula*

Widespread, common epiphyte found on the trunks and larger branches of ironbarks. White feathery flowers contrasting strongly with the dark bark of the host tree arise from clumps of thick, dumpy pseudobulbs. FLOWERING: Aug–Oct. *Dendrobium aemulum.*

SIZE/ID: Pseudobulbs 50–180 x 7–12mm. Leaves 2–4, 20–50 x 20–30mm. Racemes 30–60mm long. Flowers Aug–Oct, 2–7, 17–20 x 20–25mm.

RANGE/HABITAT: Qld, NSW (Calliope to Tanja). Coast, ranges. Open forest.

TOM CATS, ONION ORCHID *Cestichis reflexa*

Although small, the yellowish/green flowers of this lithophyte produce an unpleasant, acrid odour that resembles tom cats' urine. Clumping on rocks and cliff faces, the plants have short rounded leafy pseudobulbs, the flowers arising on racemes with the new growth. FLOWERING: Feb–Jun. PKA *Liparis reflexa*.

SIZE/ID: Leaves 100–300 x 30–35mm. Racemes 100–300mm long. Flowers 5–30, 10–15 x 8–10mm.

RANGE/HABITAT: NSW (Hastings R. to Bega). Coast, mountains. Shady humid forest.

COMMON SNOUT ORCHID *Dienia ophrydis*

Tropical terrestrial orchid with biennial stems that are leafy for a single season, supporting a long stiffly erect spike of numerous, crowded, tiny, green/brown/reddish flowers. FLOWERING: Dec–Apr.

SIZE/ID: Pseudobulbs 2, to 200 x 20mm. Leaves 3–6, 100–300 x 50–90mm. Racemes 150–300mm long. Flowers 5–6 x 5–6mm.

RANGE/HABITAT: NT (n), Qld (Cape York to Airlie Beach). Coast, ranges, tlnds. Rainforest, wetter forest, swamp margins, track verges.

HOBGOBLIN ORCHID *Empusa habenarina*

This summer-/wet season-growing terrestrial has prominently veined pale green leaves and winged flower stems carrying small green/brown/reddish flowers with narrow tepals and sharply recurved labellum. FLOWERING: Jan–Apr.

SIZE/ID: Pseudobulbs two, to 30 x 25mm. Leaves 2–3, 100–250 x 25–40mm. Racemes 200–600mm long. Flowers 8–22, 10–12 x 5–6mm.

RANGE/HABITAT: WA (n), NT (n), Qld, NSW (Torres Strait R. to Coffs Harbour). Coast, ranges, tlnds. Grassland, grassy forest.

GREEN FAIRY ORCHID *Oberonia complanata*

Clumping epiphytic orchid with fan-like growths, each consisting of 4–6 flat, fleshy, yellow/green leaves. Whorls of tiny greenish/cream flowers are densely crowded on arching/pendulous racemes. Labellum is fringed with tiny teeth. Grows on rocks and trees in shade and bright light. FLOWERING: Feb–Jul.

SIZE/ID: Leaves 80–150 x 15mm. Racemes 100–200mm long. Flowers c.2.5 x 1.8mm.

RANGE/HABITAT: Qld, NSW (Gympie to Lismore), LHI. Coast, mountains. Humid forest.

RATTLE BEAKS *Lyperanthus serratus* (left)

BROWN BEAKS *Lyperanthus suaveolens* (right)

Similar spring-flowering orchids on opposite sides of the continent, each with a single long narrow leaf and stiff racemes of long-lasting dull-coloured flowers with narrow spreading tepals. Forest/woodland, heath.

L. serratus: Leaf to 400 x 15mm. Flowers 3–10. Labellum with brush-like cluster of narrow calli. WA (Gingin to Israelite Bay). Coast, inland.

L. suaveolens: Leaf to 200 x 12mm. Flowers 2–8. Labellum with flat round calli. Qld, NSW, ACT, Vic, Tas, SA. Coast to ranges. Flowers strongly scented.

RED BEAKS, UNDERTAKER ORCHID

Pyrorchis nigricans

Large spreading colonies of this orchid flower en masse in the first year after a hot summer fire. The nodding flowers which emerge from large bracts are mostly white with red stripes and bars. FLOWERING: Aug–Nov.

SIZE/ID: Plants 100–300mm tall. Leaf single, prostrate, fleshy, green, often with black marks, 25–130 x 40–80mm. Flowers 1–8, 20–30 x 30–40mm.

RANGE/HABITAT: NSW, Vic, Tas, SA, WA. Coast, inland. Mallee, forest, heath.

RIBBED SHIELD ORCHID *Nervilia holochila*

Winter-dormant tubers of this colony-forming tropical terrestrial sprout after early summer rains to form either a broad dark green ribbed leaf or a fleshy pinkish flower stem carrying green/pink/brown flowers with a prominent pink/mauve labellum. FLOWERING: Nov–Dec.

SIZE/ID: Leaf to 200 x 80mm. Scape 150–250mm tall. Flowers 2–6, c. 4 x 3mm.

RANGE/HABITAT: WA (n), NT (n), Qld (Torres Strait to Bowen); also NG. Coast, ranges. Rainforest margins, grassy forest, swamps.

COMMON REIN ORCHID *Pecteilis propinquior*

Tropical ground orchid flowering during the summer wet season. Plants have a group of basal leaves and white scentless flowers on a stiff scape. Thin, thread-like labellum side lobes spread outwards and upwards like a pair of arms. FLOWERING: Dec–Apr. PKA *Habenaria propinquior*.

SIZE/ID: Leaves 2–4, fleshy, green, 40–80 x 8–15mm. Flowers 10–30, 12–14 x 10–12mm.

RANGE/HABITAT: Qld (Torres Strait to Rockhampton). Coast, hinterland. Paperbark woodland, wet heath, grassy forest.

DENSE MIDGE ORCHID *Corunastylis densa*

One of a group of small cryptic orchids which have the leaf blade extending stiffly outwards from the base of the spike and densely crowded nodding flowers, usually dark purple to purple/brown, occas. greenish. FLOWERING: Dec–Feb.

SIZE/ID: Plants 60–120mm tall. Leaf blade 10–18mm long. Spike 8–15mm long. Flowers 5–30, c.4.5 x 3mm.

RANGE/HABITAT: NSW (Blue Mtns to Nowra), Vic (e). Coast, mountains. Montane heath, heathy forest, rock sheets.

FRINGED MIDGE ORCHID *Corunastylis fimbriata*

Slender orchid with red-striped greenish flowers and reddish labellum that vibrates in the slightest breeze. Most segments of the flowers, which often have lemony fragrance, are fringed with coarse pink/red hairs. FLOWERING: Jan–May.

SIZE/ID: Plants 200–350mm tall. Leaf blade 20–30mm long. Spike 10–60mm long. Flowers 5–30, c.12 x 10mm.

RANGE/HABITAT: Qld, NSW (Noosa to Vincentia). Coast, mountains. Forest/ woodland, heath, rock sheets.

TINY MIDGE ORCHID *Corunastylis nuda*

Cryptic orchid which is often difficult to see in the grassy habitats where it grows. The tiny green and red/purplish flowers are densely crowded in a spike. Plants elongate up to 15cm tall after flowering to aid seed dispersal. FLOWERING: Dec–Mar.

SIZE/ID: Plants 150–300mm tall. Leaf blade 10–20mm long. Spike 25–35mm long. Flowers 5–40, c.4.5 x 3mm.

RANGE/HABITAT: NSW, ACT, Vic, Tas; also NZ. Coast, mountains. Montane/ subalpine grassland, heathy forest, swamp margins.

GREEN MIDGE ORCHID *Corunastylis pumila*

Widespread, but localised orchid found in a wide range of habitats but often difficult to see. The nodding flowers, which are often densely crowded in the spike, are green to yellowish/green, sometimes marked with red. FLOWERING: Jan–Apr.

SIZE/ID: Plants 100–200mm tall. Leaf blade 12–16mm long. Spike 15–25mm long. Flowers 5–25, c.5 x 3mm.

RANGE/HABITAT: Qld, NSW, ACT, Vic, Tas; also NZ. Coast to mountains. Heath, coastal scrub, forest, swamp margins, buttongrass moorland.

HUNCHBACK ORCHID *Corunastylis striata*

Enigmatic orchid with a thin wiry stem and smallish, maroon-striped, green/brown flowers which have a narrow, white, recurved labellum with wavy margins and deeply grooved callus plate. Often found on sandstone ledges and in moss pads. Flowers have a strong musty scent. FLOWERING: Mar–Jun.

SIZE/ID: Plants 100–250mm tall. Leaf blade 25–70mm long, erect. Spike 10–50mm long. Flowers 2–12, 7–8 x 4–5mm.

RANGE/HABITAT: NSW (Bulahdelah to Batemans Bay). Coast, hinterland ranges. Heathy forest, moist depressions.

BRITTLE MIDGE ORCHID *Genoplesium baueri*

Remarkable cryptic orchid with a brittle, fleshy, green/brown flower stem and green/brown flowers with long, widely spreading lateral sepals and a tiny red/purple labellum. Occurs mostly as single plants, occas. in crowded tufts. Flowers best after fire. FLOWERING: Feb–Apr.

SIZE/ID: Plants 50–180mm tall. Leaf blade 10–20mm long. Spike 10–25mm long. Flowers 1–12, 8–11 x 11–15(–20)mm.

RANGE/HABITAT: NSW (Kuringai Chase to Ulladulla). Coast, hinterland ranges. Forest, heath, rock sheets.

TINY ONION ORCHID *Microtideum atratum*

Widely distributed across areas of southern Australia, this small orchid grows in dense colonies in wet habitats, often in shallow water, sometimes even completely submerged. The pale-coloured plants with crowded, tiny yellow/green flowers are noticeable in dark surroundings. Flowers best after fire. FLOWERING: Sep–Dec.

SIZE/ID: Plants 50–120mm tall. Leaf blade 20–50mm long. Spike 12–35mm long. Flowers 2–40, c.2 x 2mm.

RANGE/HABITAT: Vic, Tas, SA, WA. Coast, inland. Swamps, wet flats, wet heath.

SLENDER ONION ORCHID *Microtis parviflora* (left)

COMMON ONION ORCHID *Microtis unifolia* (right)

Two commonly confused orchids. Both flower Oct–Jan and can have a spike of up to 80 or more, similar small green flowers. Qld, NSW, ACT, Vic, Tas, SA. Forest, grassland, heath, pasture, wet sites.

M. parviflora has flowers c.2 x 2mm, heart-shaped labellum with smooth margins, entire tip and no obvious apical callus.

M. unifolia has flowers to 4 x 3mm, oblong labellum with crinkled margins, notched tip and prominent apical callus.

MAUVE LEEK ORCHID *Paraprasophyllum alpestre*

Prominent in alpine/subalpine habitats, this handsome orchid can be recognised by its short, dense spikes of crowded, unscented, green/brown to purple/brown flowers with mauve bands in the petals and crystalline white labellum recurved sharply near the middle. FLOWERING: Jan–Mar.

SIZE/ID: Plants 250–450mm tall. Leaf blade to 100 x 8mm. Spike 30–80mm long. Flowers 5–25, 10–15 x 10–15mm.

RANGE/HABITAT: NSW, ACT, Vic. Mountains above 1,000m alt. Grassland, herbfields, snowgum woodland.

SHORT-LIPPED LEEK ORCHID

Paraprasophyllum brevilabre

Commonest in the season after a fire, this orchid has a short leaf blade and distinctive pale to dark flowers in which the lateral sepals are fused together and the intensely white labellum recurves sharply back on itself. FLOWERING: Aug–Jan.

SIZE/ID: Plants 200–500mm tall. Leaf blade to 100 x 7mm. Spike 80–200mm long. Flowers 8–22, 10–14 x 7–10mm.

RANGE/HABITAT: Qld (n to Gympie), NSW, ACT, Vic, Tas. Coast, mountains. Forest/woodland, heath, swamps.

LAUGHING LEEK ORCHID *Paraprasophyllum gracile*

Common, widespread, short leek orchid that often grows in tufts of several plants. Found in a wide range of habitats but often prominent in low grassy/sedgy vegetation. The variably coloured flowers are sweetly scented. Flowers without fire. FLOWERING: Jul–Nov.

SIZE/ID: Plants 60–150mm tall. Leaf blade to 150 x 2mm. Spike 80–250mm long. Flowers 5–30, 7–10 x 5mm.

RANGE/HABITAT: WA (Shark Bay to Israelite Bay). Coast, inland. Sparse/shrubby forest, rock outcrops, wet flats.

SCENTED LEEK ORCHID *Paraprasophyllum odoratum*

Originally thought to be widely distributed in se Australia, this leek orchid can be distinguished by the relatively large fragrant flowers, widely spreading lateral sepals, crinkly labellum recurved at more than right angles and green callus extending just past the labellum bend. FLOWERING: Oct–Nov.

SIZE/ID: Plants 300–800mm tall. Leaf blade to 150 x 6mm. Spike 60–100mm long. Flowers 8–35, 13–17 x 9–12mm.

RANGE/HABITAT: Vic (w), SA. Coast, ranges. Forest/ woodland, heath.

TALL LEEK ORCHID *Prasophyllum elatum*

Widespread, common orchid with crowded, yellowish/greenish/brownish or purplish lightly scented flowers, each with a broad curved labellum with crinkled margins. Flowers strongly after fire, occas. in unburnt habitat. Whole plants occas. blackish.

FLOWERING: Aug–Dec.

SIZE/ID: Plants 800–1,600mm tall. Leaf blade to 200 x 15mm. Spike 200–400mm long. Flowers 15–60(–100), 10–15 x 7–10mm.

RANGE/HABITAT: Qld (n to Fraser Is.), NSW, Vic, Tas, SA, WA. Coast, mountains, rare inland. Forest/woodland, mallee, heath.

YELLOW LEEK ORCHID *Prasophyllum flavum*

Distinctive leek orchid which can be recognised by its short stiff leaf blade (often purplish) and yellow/green flowers with strong spicy scent. Flowers without fire but much easier to see on burnt ground. FLOWERING: Oct–Feb.

SIZE/ID: Plants 400–900mm tall. Leaf blade to 300 x 5mm. Spike 80–200mm long. Flowers 6–50(–70), 8–10 x 8–10mm.

RANGE/HABITAT: Qld (s), NSW, Vic, Tas (Flinders Is., King Is.). Coast, mountains. Higher rainfall forest, heathy forest, coastal scrub.

KING LEEK ORCHID *Prasophyllum regium*

Australia's tallest orchid. Sturdy plants with crowded yellow/green to purple/brown, lightly scented flowers, the curved labellum in each flower with weakly crinkled margins and a large protruding callus plate. Flowers strongly after fire. FLOWERING: Sep–Dec.

SIZE/ID: Plants 500–2,000mm tall. Leaf blade to 250 x 15mm. Spike 100–500mm long. Flowers 40–100, 16–25 x 10–15mm.

RANGE/HABITAT: WA (Perth to Albany). Mainly near-coastal areas. Wet flats, swamps, high-rainfall forest.

EASTERN UNDERGROUND ORCHID *Rhizanthella slateri*

Remarkable cryptic orchid that spends its entire life cycle underground. Leafless and rootless, the plants consist of fleshy rhizomes that spread, branch, and form specialised heads of flowers to 30mm wide that mature just below soil level. Most discoveries are accidental. FLOWERING: Aug–Nov.

SIZE/ID: Rhizomes to 40 x 15mm, white. Flowers tubular, 15–30 per head, to 8 x 3mm, pink/purple, facing inwards in spiral rows. Fruit fleshy, ripening yellow.

RANGE/HABITAT: NSW (Bulahdelah to Jervis Bay, Blue Mtns). Coast, mountains. Forest/woodland.

BLACK-STRIPED LEAFY GREENHOOD

Bunochilus longifolius (left)

TUNSTALL'S LEAFY GREENHOOD

Bunochilus tunstallii (right)

Winter-/spring-flowering dimorphic greenhoods which have green hooded flowers with darker stripes. Flower open at front with deflexed lower lip; labellum exposed, with basal mound and upturned notched tip. Sterile plant is a rosette. Forest/woodland.

B. longifolius 150–500mm tall, 1–11 flowers, labellum hairy, pale green with blackish stripe and mound. NSW. AKA *Pterostylis longifolia*.

B. tunstallii 250–500mm tall, 3–10 flowers, labellum dark brown with darker stripe and mound. NSW, Vic, Tas. AKA *Pterostylis tustallii*.

SCARLET GREENHOOD *Diplodium coccinum*

Large-flowered, dimorphic, summer-/autumn-flowering greenhood with bluish/green, reddish/green or red and white flowers, the hood bending in a long, graceful curve and the labellum protruding prominently from the sinus. Grows in colonies, often on sheltered slopes or among rocks. FLOWERING: Jan–Apr. AKA *Pterostylis coccina.*

SIZE/ID: Rosette separate; leaves to 30 x 15mm. Stem to 22cm tall. Flower 1, to 50 x 19mm.

RANGE/HABITAT: NSW, ACT, Vic (ne). Mountains. Shrubby/grassy forest.

COBRA GREENHOOD, SUPERB GREENHOOD

Diplodium grandiflorum

Winter-/spring-flowering dimorphic greenhood with spectacular flowers. Easily recognised by the broadly flared, red/brown petals flanking the gracefully curved hood and the narrow labellum with swollen knob-like apex. Rosettes of non-flowering plants have crinkled margins. FLOWERING: Apr–Aug. AKA *Pterostylis grandiflora*.

SIZE/ID: Rosette separate; leaves to 20 x 10mm. Stem to 40cm tall. Flower 1, to 35 x 23mm.

RANGE/HABITAT: Qld (n to Gympie, NSW, Vic, Tas (ne). Coast, mountains. Wetter forest, heathy forest.

BRITTLE GREENHOOD, LITTLE DUMPIES

Diplodium truncatum

Short-growing, dimorphic, summer-/winter-flowering greenhood with large, dumpy green and white or brown and white semi-nodding flowers with blunt downcurved apex to the hood, broad petals, and curved, shortly protruding labellum. Often grows in extensive colonies. FLOWERING: Jan–Apr. AKA *Pterostylis truncata.*

SIZE/ID: Rosette separate; leaves to 30 x 18mm. Stem to 15cm tall. Flower 1, to 45 x 20mm.

RANGE/HABITAT: NSW, ACT, Vic. Coast, mountains. Shrubby forest, grassy forest, grassland, among rocks.

SWAN GREENHOOD *Hymenochilus cycnocephalus* (left)

MIDGET GREENHOOD *Hymenochilus muticus* (right)

Winter-/spring-flowering greenhoods with a basal rosette of fleshy leaves and small green hooded flowers. Flower open at front with cupped/pouched lower lip; labellum whitish, exposed, membranous, with dark green basal appendage. Forest/woodland, shrubland, mallee.

H. cycnocephalus 80–200mm tall, 2–12 flowers, labellum with beak-like appendage. NSW, ACT, Vic. AKA *Pterostylis cycnocephala.*

H. muticus 120–350mm tall, 2–22 flowers, labellum with recurved, tongue-like appendage. Qld, NSW, ACT, Vic, Tas. AKA *Pterostylis mutica.*

BOORMAN'S RUSTYHOOD

Oligochaetochilus boormannii

Widespread rustyhood notable for its dark reddish/brown to blackish flowers with a broad hairy synsepalum (often backswept towards the ovary) and relatively small thick, fleshy, channelled labellum adorned with numerous white bristles. FLOWERING: Sep–Nov. AKA *Pterostylis boormannii.*

SIZE/ID: Plants 50–200mm tall. Leaves 8–14, 20–30 x 6–10mm. Flowers 1–7, 25–30 x 10–12mm.

RANGE/HABITAT: Qld (s), NSW, Vic, SA. Mainly inland. Drier forest/woodland, mallee, native pines.

GAWLER RANGE RUSTYHOOD *Oligochaetochilus ovatus*

Short, sturdy, localised rustyhood with large rosette leaves and relatively large flowers that are mainly translucent white with red/brown/pink shades, wide synsepalum with thickish points and large stripey labellum with scalloped margins and numerous short bristles. FLOWERING: Sep–Oct. AKA *Pterostylis ovata*.

SIZE/ID: Plants 150–350mm tall. Leaves 3–7, 15–35 x 8–12mm. Flowers 1–6, 30–35 x 10–12mm.

RANGE/HABITAT: SA (Gawler Ra.). Sand between quartzite boulders, crevices/pockets on rock sheets.

BRISTLY RUSTYHOOD *Oligochaetochilus setifer*

Slender rustyhood with translucent white and green/brown flowers held obliquely erect on longish stalks. The thick, brown, deeply grooved, densely hairy labellum, which is projected forwards from the centre of the flower, looks remarkably like a visiting insect. FLOWERING: Sep–Dec. AKA *Pterostylis setifera*.

SIZE/ID: Plants 150–300mm tall. Leaves 6–10, 15–35 x 8–12mm. Flowers 2–10, 20–28 x 7–10mm.

RANGE/HABITAT: Qld (s), NSW, Vic, SA (se). Inland. Drier forest/ woodland, mallee, native pines.

MOORA RUSTYHOOD *Oligochaetochilus spathulatus*

Recognised by its semi-nodding flowers with a translucent, red-lined bulbous hood and shallowly pouched, red/brown lateral sepals with hairy margins. The dorsal sepal and lateral sepals all have longish filamentous tips which converge and often meet or overlap. FLOWERING: Sep–Oct. AKA *Pterostylis spathulata*.

SIZE/ID: Plants 150–350mm tall. Leaves 6–10, 20–45 x 7–14mm. Flowers 2–12, 20–22 x 7–9mm.

RANGE/HABITAT: WA (Mullewa to Fitzgerald R.). Mainly inland. Woodland, shrubland, granite outcrops.

LONG-TAILED RUSTYHOOD *Oligochaetochilus woollsii*

The long, dangling, thread-like sepal tips of this impressive orchid and its large, beaked labellum, are unique features in native orchids. Although widespread, it mostly occurs in small, scattered populations. FLOWERING: Oct–Dec. AKA *Pterostylis woollsii*.

SIZE/ID: Plants 250–400mm tall. Leaves 5–10, 15–40 x 8–20mm. Flowers 1–6, 250–350 x 8–12mm.

RANGE/HABITAT: Qld (n to Carnarvon Gorge), NSW, Vic (near Rushworth). Mainly inland, rare near coast. Rock outcrops, ridges, hilltops. Drier forest/woodland.

DAINTREY'S GREENHOOD *Pharochilum daintreanum*

Tall, slender, dimorphic greenhood with narrow, translucent, white and dark green hooded flowers, obliquely deflexed lateral sepals and an exposed, 3-lobed, dark brown/blackish labellum with large side lobes and no basal lobe. Sterile plant is a rosette. FLOWERING: Jan–Jul. AKA *Pterostylis daintreana.*

SIZE/ID: Plants 100–300mm tall. Leaves 3–5, closely sheathing, bract-like. Flowers 1–7, 14–17 x 4–5mm.

RANGE/HABITAT: Qld (s), NSW. Coast, mountains. Forest/woodland, shrubland, heath, often among rocks.

BIRD ORCHID *Plumatichilos barbatus*

Common greenhood with an extended rosette of overlapping green leaves with pale areas and netted veins. Bulging hooded flowers marked with dark green netted veins and brown frontal areas have widely splayed lateral sepals and a thin sparsely hairy labellum with a small brown apical knob. FLOWERING: Jul–Sep. AKA *Pterostylis barbata*.

SIZE/ID: Leaves 10–25 in basal rosette, to 45 x 12mm. Stem to 400mm tall. Flower 1, to 65 x 14mm.

RANGE/HABITAT: WA (Bindoon to Albany). Coast, inland. Forest/woodland, shrubland, sheoak groves.

BEARDED GREENHOOD *Plumatichilos plumosus*

Sturdy greenhood with shiny green flowers netted with darker green veins, short thick tip on the hood, green petals, thick channelled lateral sepals held close together and a thin protruding labellum covered with bright yellow hairs and with a thick brown apical knob. FLOWERING: Aug–Oct. AKA *Pterostylis plumosa*.

SIZE/ID: Leaves 10–20 in basal rosette, to 45 x 12mm. Stem to 200mm tall. Flower 1, to 45 x 10mm.

RANGE/HABITAT: NSW (Alectown to Mangoplah). Inland ranges and slopes. Forest/woodland.

KING GREENHOOD *Pterostylis baptistii*

Imposing greenhood recognised by its large, upright flower with strongly bulging sinus and long, curved, pointed labellum. Locally common in clonal colonies. Spectacular in flower. Autumn- and winter-flowering populations occur. FLOWERING: Mar–May, Aug–Nov.

SIZE/ID: Leaves 4–8 in basal rosette, to 8 x 2.5cm, margins wavy/crinkled. Stem to 40cm tall. Flower 1, to 60 x 30mm, white and green, apex brown.

RANGE/HABITAT: Qld, NSW, Vic (e). Coast, ranges. Wetter forests, forest margins, swamp margins.

LEAFY GREENHOOD *Pterostylis cucullata*

Distinctive orchid recognised by its fleshy rosette leaves and large semi-nodding flower with short horns that extend just above the hood, the brown front of the flower with a velvety appearance. Usually found in small clonal groups. Now uncommon and rare. FLOWERING: Aug–Oct.

SIZE/ID: Leaves 5–7, upper leaf often sheathing flower, to 10 x 3cm, margins smooth/crinkled. Stem to 10cm tall. Flower 1, to 40 x 25mm.

RANGE/HABITAT: Vic (s), Tas, SA (se). Coastal/near coastal. Heath, scrub.

BLUNT GREENHOOD *Pterostylis curta*

Popular orchid recognised by its single, upright flower and strongly twisted labellum that just protrudes from the front opening. Grows in clonal colonies, sometimes large and often crowded. Widespread, common.
FLOWERING: Jul–Oct.

SIZE/ID: Leaves 3–6 in basal rosette, to 10 x 3cm, margins smooth/crinkled. Stem to 30cm tall, occas. quite short. Flower 1, to 35 x 15mm, green, white and brownish.

RANGE/HABITAT: Qld, NSW, LHI, ACT, Vic, Tas, SA. Coast, mountains, inland slopes. Forest/woodland, heath.

NODDING GREENHOOD *Pterostylis nutans*

Familiar orchid with a strongly nodding flower and curved hairy labellum protruding from the front. Often seen growing in large colonies, the flowers sometimes almost glowing. Popular with adults and children. Widespread, common. FLOWERING: Mar–Dec.

SIZE/ID: Rosette leaves 3–6, to 9 x 3cm, margins wavy/crinkled. Stem to 30cm tall, occas. quite short. Flower to 25 x 14mm, translucent green with darker lines.

RANGE/HABITAT: Qld, NSW, ACT, Vic, Tas, SA; also NZ. Coast, mountains, inland slopes. Forest/woodland, heath.

TINY GREENHOOD *Speculantha parviflora* (left)

MARSH GREENHOOD *Speculantha uliginosa* (right)

Tiny greenhoods have multiple, small, closed flowers that face inwards towards the scape, the labellum mostly hidden within the flower.

S. parviflora 50–250mm tall, flowers 1–8, green and white, tip often brown. Qld, NSW, Vic, Tas, SA (se). Coast to ranges. Forest, heath. FLOWERING: Jun–Nov. AKA *Pterostylis parviflora.*

S. uliginosa 60–150mm tall, flowers 1–7 on plump ovaries, shiny, green and white. NSW, Vic, Tas, SA. Coast to mountains. Swamps. FLOWERING: Feb–May. AKA *Pterostylis uliginosa.*

JUG ORCHID *Stamnorchis recurva*

Unique native orchid immediately recognised by its unusual, strongly striped, tubular, jug-like flowers which are open at the top, with petal tips hooked outwards and abruptly recurved terete points on the lateral sepals. FLOWERING: Aug–Oct. AKA *Pterostylis recurva*.

SIZE/ID: Plants 200–900mm tall. Leaves 6–15, 30–50 x 8–12mm. Flowers 1–5, 30–35 x 13–16mm.

RANGE/HABITAT: WA (Geraldton to Israelite Bay). Coast, inland. Forest/woodland, mallee, shrubland, granite outcrops.

RED BANDED GREENHOOD *Urochilus sanguineus* (left)

GREEN BANDED GREENHOOD *Urochilus vittatus* (right)

Banded greenhoods have hooded flowers with darker bands. Flower open at front with broad, deflexed lower lip; labellum exposed, with tail-like appendage. Sterile plant a rosette.

U. sanguineus 150–400mm tall, flowers 2–15, dark red/brown with darker bands. Vic, Tas, SA, WA. Coast to hills. FLOWERING: Jun–Oct. AKA *Pterostylis sanguinea*.

U. vittatus 200–450mm tall, flowers 2–25, green with darker bands. WA (Dongara to Esperance). Coast to wheatbelt, granite outcrops. FLOWERING: Apr–Sep. AKA *Pterostylis vittata*.

PINK SPIRAL ORCHID *Spiranthes australis*

Common ground orchid with closely spaced colourful flowers arranged spirally in a spike. The scentless flowers, usually in tones of pink with a white labellum, contain nectar which attracts insects to feed. FLOWERING: Oct–Mar.

SIZE/ID: Leaves 3–5, fleshy, green, 80–160 x 6–10mm. Flowers 10–50, 4–5 x 2.5–3mm.

RANGE/HABITAT: Qld (s), NSW, Vic, Tas, SA. Coast, ranges, inland slopes. Moist/wet soil in swamps, streambanks, grassy/heathy forest.

COPPER BEARD ORCHID, BUSHRANGER ORCHID

Calochilus campestris

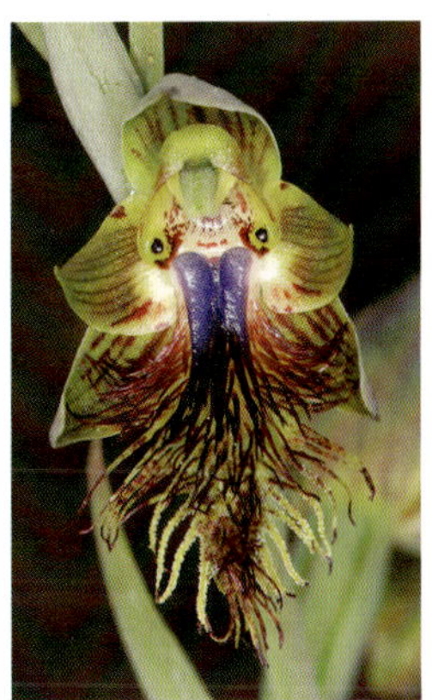

The commonest of a group of beard orchids with a curved labellum (when viewed from the side), the labellum base covered with smooth metallic plates (often bluish) and the main part covered with stiff red/purple hairs and resembling a bristly beard. FLOWERING: Sep–Jan.

SIZE/ID: Leaf 150–350 x 10–15mm. Scape 300–600mm tall. Flowers 5–15, 18–22 x 12–16mm.

RANGE/HABITAT: Qld, NSW, Vic, Tas (Bass Strait Is.). Coast, ranges. Heath, forest, swamps.

GIANT BEARD ORCHID *Calochilus grandiflorus*

Impressive beard orchid with large colourful flowers, usually golden/ bronze with red lines (prominent on the petals) and a broad bearded labellum thickly covered with red hairs. The labellum ends in a long, naked, strap-like tail and the column has two prominent eye-spots.
FLOWERING: Sep–Dec.

SIZE/ID: Leaf 300–600 x 5–8mm. Scape 300–600mm tall. Flowers 1–15, 35–45 x 22–28mm.

RANGE/HABITAT: Qld, NSW (Fraser Is. to Gosford). Coast, mountains. Heath, forest, swamp margins.

RED BEARD ORCHID *Calochilus paludosus*

Distinctive beard orchid recognised by its yellow/green flowers with red/bronze stripes and the labellum covered with coarse, red, glistening hairs and ending in a naked strap-like tail. The colourful flowers open extra widely on hot sunny days. FLOWERING: Sep–Jan.

SIZE/ID: Leaf 100–180 x 4–7mm. Scape 150–350mm tall. Flowers 1–9, 28–34 x 10–14mm.

RANGE/HABITAT: Qld (s), NSW, ACT, Vic, Tas, SA. Coast, mountains, inland. Forest/woodland, heath, swamp margins.

PURPLE BEARD ORCHID *Calochilus robertsonii*

Beard orchid with yellow/green flowers heavily marked with red stripes, the labellum covered with coarse purple hairs and ending in a short, narrow, squiggly, glandular tail. Two eye-spots adorn the base of the column. FLOWERING: Sep–Jan.

SIZE/ID: Leaf 150–400 x 8–15mm. Scape 150–300mm tall. Flowers 1–9, 28–34 x 10–14mm.

RANGE/HABITAT: Recorded from Qld, NSW, ACT, Vic, Tas, SA but exact range uncertain. Coast, mountains, inland. Forest/woodland, heath.

BABE-IN-A-CRADLE *Epiblema grandiflorum*

The broad labellum of this distinctive orchid has two ridges at the base adorned with curious ribbon-like appendages and the column is hooded by a pair of unusual, blue-spotted wings. The widely opening bright blue/mauve flowers are also spotted and streaked with darker markings. FLOWERING: Nov–Jan.

SIZE/ID: Leaf 150–300 x 4–5mm, terete, hollow. Scape 300–1,000mm tall. Flowers 2–8, 25–40mm across.

RANGE/HABITAT: WA (Gingin to Esperance). Mainly coastal. Swamps, often in standing water.

RABBIT EARS, VANILLA ORCHID *Thelymitra antennifera*

Common sun orchid that grows in colonies. Plants have a narrow dark green leaf, thin, wiry scape and pale lemon-yellow flowers, the cream/yellow column supporting two prominent dark brown ear-like lobes. The long-lasting vanilla-scented flowers open freely, even on cool days. FLOWERING: Jul–Nov.

SIZE/ID: Leaf 50–180 x 2–3mm. Scape 150–300m tall. Flowers 2–40, 20–35mm across.

RANGE/HABITAT: Vic, Tas, SA, WA. Coast, ranges, inland. Coastal scrub, heath, heathy forest, woodland, mallee.

GREAT SUN ORCHID *Thelymitra aristata*

Robust sun orchid with a large thick fleshy leaf, large stem bracts and an amazing display of pleasantly scented deep bluish/purple flowers lightly marked with darker veins. Relatively long-lasting, the flowers, open readily on warm to hot days. **FLOWERING:** Sep–Nov.

SIZE/ID: Leaf 100–400 x 5–40mm. Scape 200–1,000m tall. Flowers 2–40, 20–45mm across.

RANGE/HABITAT: NSW (se), Vic, Tas, SA (se). Coast, adjacent ranges. Heath, heathy forest, open forest, swamp margins.

LEOPARD SUN ORCHID *Thelymitra benthamiana*

Easily identified sun orchid with a short broad leaf, yellow/green flowers with reddish blotches and a distinctive column which has a deeply fringed apical mantle that resembles a jumping spider. The strongly marked flowers open mainly on hot humid days. FLOWERING: Sep–Dec.

SIZE/ID: Leaf 50–150 x 20–35mm. Scape 150–500m tall. Flowers 1–15, 25–40mm across.

RANGE/HABITAT: Vic, Tas (Flinders Is.), SA, WA. Coast, adjacent ranges. Heath, open forest, mallee, swamp margins.

BLUE LADY ORCHID *Thelymitra crinita*

The brilliant sky-blue flowers of this western sun orchid, which open freely on hot sunny days, produce an impressive floral display. This distinctive orchid can also be recognised by its short broad leaf, crested column apex and the labellum being distinctly narrower than the other segments.

FLOWERING: Sep–Dec.

SIZE/ID: Leaf 50–150 x 10–45mm. Scape 200–650m tall. Flowers 2–20, 30–45mm across.

RANGE/HABITAT: WA (Bindoon to Israelite Bay). Coast, inland. Forest/ woodland, scrub.

SPOTTED SUN ORCHID *Thelymitra ixioides* (left)

LARGE-SPOTTED SUN ORCHID *Thelymitra juncifolia* (right)

Two confusing common orchids found in shrubby forest and heath. Both flower Sep–Dec and have similar blue/mauve flowers with dark spots/dots on the dorsal sepal and petals.

T. ixioides has small dark spots/dots (occas. no spots at all), column with short, finger-like papillae and dense hair tufts. Qld, NSW, Vic, Tas, SA. Coast, mountains, inland slopes.

T. juncifolia has less-defined but larger spots, column with longer, finger-like papillae and sparse hair tufts. NSW, Vic, Tas, SA. Coast, hills.

LARGE-LEAVED SUN ORCHID *Thelymitra macrophylla*

Robust western sun orchid with a broad, thick, ribbed leaf, large stem bracts and freely opening blue flowers (occas. pink or white) with broad, pointed tepals and large pale column which has a narrow black and yellow apical lobe and white hair tufts. FLOWERING: Aug–Nov.

SIZE/ID: Leaf 150–500 x 20–40mm. Scape 300–1,000m tall. Flowers 5–30, 20–50mm across.

RANGE/HABITAT: WA (Perth to Bremer Bay). Coast, inland. Forest/woodland.

SPIRAL SUN ORCHID *Thelymitra matthewsii*

Uncommon sun orchid with a spirally twisted leaf and relatively small, short-lasting, upward-facing, dark purple flowers with darker veins and yellow ear-like column lobes. The flowers open more widely on hot sunny days. Flowers best after fire and much easier to see on burnt ground. FLOWERING: Aug–Oct.

SIZE/ID: Leaf 30–70 x 3–7mm. Scape 90–150m tall. Flowers 1(–2), 15–25mm across.

RANGE/HABITAT: Vic, SA; also NZ. Coast, adjacent hills. Heath, heathy forest.

SLENDER SUN ORCHID *Thelymitra pauciflora*

The short-lasting self-pollinating pale blue flowers (occas. pink) of this slender sun orchid open tardily, usually expanding widely only on hot humid days. In cool seasons the flowers may not open at all. The column has a narrow yellow top and upcurved dense mop-like hair tufts. FLOWERING: Sep–Nov.

SIZE/ID: Leaf 100–300 x 3–6mm. Scape 100–350m tall. Flowers 1–3(–5), 15–20mm across.

RANGE/HABITAT: Qld (s), NSW, ACT, Vic, Tas, SA. Coast, mountains. Heath, heathy forest, open forest, grassland.

SALMON SUN ORCHID *Thelymitra rubra*

Common, slender sun orchid with thin, wiry, flexuose stems and smallish reddish to reddish/pink self-pollinating flowers that open freely on warm to hot days. Often grows in crowded tufts of multiple plants. Flowers best after summer fires. FLOWERING: Aug–Dec.

SIZE/ID: Leaf 50–70 x 2–3mm. Scape 100–400m tall. Flowers 1–5, 18–25mm across.

RANGE/HABITAT: NSW, ACT, Vic, Tas, SA. Coast, ranges, inland. Various habitats, especially heath and heathy forest.

QUEEN OF SHEBA *Thelymitra variegata*

The gaudy colour combinations and iridescence of the floral parts make this sun orchid unrivalled in the world of orchids. The flowers, which open widely on warm sunny days, are basically in reddish, purplish or violet colours marked with blotches and streaks of orange, red, yellow and pink. FLOWERING: Aug–Oct.

SIZE/ID: Leaf 50–150 x 5–10mm. Scape 150–350m tall. Flowers 1–6, 30–55mm across.

RANGE/HABITAT: WA (Perth to Albany). Coast, uncommon inland. Heath, heathy forest, woodland.

BEETLE ORCHID *Peristeranthus hillii*

Large, sparsely branched tropical/subtropical epiphyte. Relatively large drooping leaves and long, narrow, pendulous racemes with small, fragrant, forward-facing, crimson-spotted, green flowers characterise the species.

FLOWERING: Aug–Nov.

SIZE/ID: Stems 100–300mm long. Leaves 3–10, 150–250 x 30–40mm. Racemes 100–150mm long, multiflowered. Flowers 6–8 x 5–7mm.

RANGE/HABITAT: Qld, NSW (Bloomfield R. to Port Macquarie). Coast, ranges, tlnds. Rainforest, vine thickets, wet lowland forests.

NATIVE MOTH ORCHID *Phalaenopsis rosenstromii*

Sporadically distributed and rarely encountered, this epiphyte has large, white, moth-like flowers and narrow labellum with two curved thread-like appendages. The plants can be recognised by their short stems, long cord-like roots and large leathery leaves. FLOWERING: Dec–Apr.

SIZE/ID: Stems 100–300mm long. Leaves 2–8, 150–300 x 40–70mm. Panicles 300–750mm long. Flowers 2–10, 60–70 x 50–80mm.

RANGE/HABITAT: Qld (Iron Ra. to Paluma Ra.); also NG. Ranges. Wetter forests, often near streams and waterfalls.

TANGLE ORCHID, TANGLE ROOT *Plectorrhiza tridentata*

Widely distributed spreading/dangling epiphyte with the plant supported on the host by just a few roots, most roots forming an aerial tangle. Often seen on trees and shrubs in shady, humid gullies and near streams. FLOWERING: Sep–Jan.

SIZE/ID: Stems 100–300mm long. Leaves 3–12, 50–100 x 10–15mm. Racemes 50–120mm long. Flowers 3–15, 5–6 x 6–8mm, strongly scented.

RANGE/HABITAT: Qld, NSW, Vic (Windsor Tlnd to Orbost). Coast, ranges/tlnds. Rainforest, wetter forests, streambanks.

BUTTERFLY ORCHID *Sarcochilus australis*

Small epiphyte, usually unbranched, with numerous roots, spreading leaves and pendulous racemes with widely spaced flowers, often green but sometimes brown, with narrow tepals and a prominent white labellum. Often grows in localised patches. FLOWERING: Oct–Dec.

SIZE/ID: Stems 20–50mm long. Leaves 3–10, 40–80 x 10–14mm. Racemes 70–160mm long. Flowers 2–14, 16–22 x 12–15mm.

RANGE/HABITAT: NSW (n to Kyogle), Vic, Tas. Coast, adjacent ranges. Rainforest, humid thickets, gullies.

ORANGE-BLOSSOM ORCHID *Sarcochilus falcatus*

Showy when in flower, this widely distributed epiphyte has spreading leathery leaves and striking, cream to white flowers with yellow patches and purplish stripes on the labellum. Older plants branch basally to form clumps. Flowers fragrant. FLOWERING: Jun–Nov.

SIZE/ID: Stems 30–60mm long. Leaves 3–10, 60–100 x 9–12mm. Racemes 50–100mm long. Flowers 3–12, 12–35 x 12–35mm.

RANGE/HABITAT: Qld, NSW, Vic (Cooktown to East Gippsland). Coast, ranges/tlnds. Rainforest, streambanks, ridgetops.

RAVINE ORCHID *Sarcochilus fitzgeraldii*

Shade-loving, clumping lithophyte with freely branching stems bearing upright/arching, curved, dark green leaves. White flowers, almost circular in shape, have contrasting central areas variably marked with crimson spots. The labellum is white with red bars. FLOWERING: Oct–Nov.

SIZE/ID: Stems 200–500mm long. Leaves 4–8, 100–200 x 10–15mm. Racemes 100–200mm long. Flowers 4–15, 25–35 x 25–35mm.

RANGE/HABITAT: Qld, NSW (Maleny to Carrai). Ranges/tlnds. Rainforest, cliff faces.

MYRTLE BELLS *Sarcochilus hillii*

Small epiphyte with narrow, dark green, deeply channelled leaves and small, crystalline white or pale pink flowers that open sporadically 1–3 at a time. Four bright yellow calli and massed white hairs adorn the labellum. FLOWERING: Oct–Dec.

SIZE/ID: Stems 20–50mm long. Leaves 2–10, 60–100 x 3mm. Racemes 50–120mm long. Flowers 2–10, 8–10 x 8–10mm.

RANGE/HABITAT: Qld, NSW (Rockhampton to near Bega). Ranges/tlnds. Humid thickets, drier humid forests.

LAWYER ORCHID *Sarcochilus olivaceus*

Usually projecting out from the host, this epiphyte has a single growth with bright green spreading leaves. Narrow green to yellowish tepals seem to stretch out widely from the greenish labellum which is marked with a few red/brown bars.

FLOWERING: Jun–Jan.

SIZE/ID: Stems 30–80mm long. Leaves 2–8, 80–150 x 20–35mm. Racemes 90–140mm long. Flowers 2–12, 18–22 x 2–25mm.

RANGE/HABITAT: Qld, NSW (Maleny to near Bega). Coast, ranges. Rainforest, streambanks.

SMALL BUTTERFLY ORCHID *Sarcochilus spathulatus*

Small epiphyte, usually unbranched, with leathery leaves often marked with purple spots. Short pendulous racemes carry widely spaced green, brown or yellowish flowers, with narrow tepals and a contrasting white labellum. FLOWERING: Jul–Oct.

SIZE/ID: Stems 20–40mm long. Leaves 2–10, 30–70 x 14–17mm. Racemes 30–50mm long. Flowers 1–8, 12–16 x 10–14mm.

RANGE/HABITAT: Qld, NSW (Bunya Mtns to Watagan Mtns). Coast, mountains. Rainforest, wetter forests.

BLOTCHED BUTTERFLY ORCHID *Sarcochilus weinthalii*

Although with a relatively wide distribution, this epiphyte is generally localised and uncommon to rare. It has showy greenish-cream flowers ornately marked with purple/reddish spots and blotches, the labellum with a distinctive dark apical spot. **FLOWERING**: Aug–Oct.

SIZE/ID: Stems 40–80mm long. Leaves 3–7, 50–90 x 10–12mm. Racemes 50–70mm long. Flowers 3–15, 12–16 x 12–15mm.

RANGE/HABITAT: Qld, NSW (Bunya Mtns to Clarence R.). Rainforest, humid thickets.

CHAIN RIBBONROOT *Taeniophyllum muelleri*

Easily overlooked, tiny leafless epiphyte with thin, greenish, photosynthetic roots and filiform racemes which carry widely spaced small tubular greenish flowers. Swollen green capsules are more conspicuous than the flowers. Often grows in spreading clumps, proliferating from root tips, with the plants linked together in chains. FLOWERING: Aug–Oct.

SIZE/ID: Stems c.1mm long. Leaves absent. Racemes 30–50mm long. Flowers 4–9, c.3 x 2mm.

RANGE/HABITAT: Qld, NSW (Cape York Pen. to Brunswick Heads). Coast, ranges. Humid forests.

CAPE YORK VANDA *Vanda hindsii*

Large epiphyte, branching from base with coarse white roots, two ranks of long strap-like leathery leaves and stiff racemes carrying large, round, shiny brown flowers with wavy green margins on the tepals and an intensely white central patch. **FLOWERING**: Sep–Mar.

SIZE/ID: Stems 500–1,000mm long. Leaves numerous, 200–400 x 30–40mm. Racemes 100–200mm long. Flowers 3–7, 30–35 x 30–35mm.

RANGE/HABITAT: Qld (Cape York Pen.); also NG, Bougainville, Solomon Is. Coast, ranges. Rainforest, granite boulders.

BOOTLACE ORCHID *Erythrorchis cassythoides*

Terrestrial orchid with blackish, unbranched, leafless, wiry stems climbing on tree trunks and supported by short unbranched roots. New stems arise as the old ones die. Fragrant yellow/brown flowers arise in large panicles each flower with a protruding tubular white labellum and lasting a few days. FLOWERING: Aug–Dec.

SIZE/ID: Stems to 6m tall. Flowers 20–25mm across.

RANGE/HABITAT: Qld, NSW (Blackdown Tlnd to Waterfall). Coast, ranges. Open sites often near decaying wood and litter in forest.

GIANT CLIMBING ORCHID *Pseudovanilla foliata*

Vigorous climbing orchid forming crowded growths on piles of decaying timber and often climbing high into trees. Thick green to yellow/orange freely branching stems with leaf-like bracts have large panicles of fragrant yellow/orange flowers, the broad labellum adorned with thick red/orange papillae. Plants die out as the timber decays. FLOWERING: Oct–Feb.

SIZE/ID: Stems to 15m tall. Flowers 30–40mm across.

RANGE/HABITAT: Qld, NSW (McIlwraith Ra to Taree). Coast, ranges. Rainforest, wetter forests and slopes. Often damaged/disturbed sites.

GLOSSARY

Acuminate With a long, drawn-out point.
Acute With a short, sharp point.
Aerial roots Adventitious roots arising on stems and growing in the air.
Axillary Borne in an axil.
Blade The expanded part of a leaf or labellum.
Bract A leaf-like structure which lacks a blade or lamina.
Bracteose Bearing prominent bracts.
Caespitose Growing in dense clumps or tufts.
Calcareous An excess of lime in a soil.
Calli Non-secreting glands found on the labellum of orchids.
Callus A fleshy ridged or plate-like structure found on the labellum.
Calyx The outer sepals of the flower.
Colonial Colony-forming.
Capsule Dry dehiscent fruit (as in orchids).
Cauline Belonging to the stem, usually referring to leaves.
Club Term used for the expanded/thickened apical part of sepals or petals.
Column The central fleshy structure in orchid flowers composed of the style and staminal filaments.
Column foot An extension of the base of the column.
Column wing A flattened often wing-like appendage on the column.
Cordate Heart-shaped.
Crinkled/crispate Irregularly waved, twisted, curled and ruffled.
Cupped Where the segments remain concave and do not become flat.
Decurved Curved downwards.

Deflexed Bent sharply downwards.
Dentate Toothed.
Dimorphic Existing in two forms.
Dissected Deeply divided into segments.
Dorsal The upper side.
Eglandular Without a gland.
Elongate Drawn out in length.
Endemic Restricted to a given region or country.
Entire Simple and undivided.
Epiphyte A plant growing on or attached to other plants, but not parasitic.
Erect Upright.
Evergreen Remaining green and retaining leaves throughout the year.
Family A taxonomic group of related genera.
Fertile bract A bract which subtends a pedicel or sessile ovary.
Filiform Thread-like.
Fimbriate Fringed along a margin.
Galea A hood or helmet-like structure formed by the fusion or close overlap of dorsal sepal and petals (for example, greenhoods).
Genus A taxonomic group of closely related species.
Glabrous Without hairs, smooth.
Glaucous Bluish to bluish-grey.
Globose Globular; almost spherical.
Habit The general appearance of a plant.
Habitat The environment in which a plant grows.
Indigenous Native to a county, region or area.
Inflorescence The flowering structure of a plant.
Insectiform Shaped like or resembling an insect.

Labellum A lip; the third petal; in orchids the modified petal in front of the flower.

Lamina The expanded part of a leaf.

Lateral Arising at the side of the main axis.

Lateral lobes The two side lobes of the labellum.

Lax Loose, drooping, non-turgid.

Leaflet Segment of a compound leaf.

Linear Long and narrow with parallel sides.

Lithophyte Plant growing on rocks, boulders or cliff faces.

Littoral Growing in communities near the sea.

Lobe A rounded or blunt segment.

Lobed Divided into lobes.

Marginal Attached to or near the edge.

Membranous Thin-textured.

Midlobe The main projecting lobe of the labellum.

Midrib The main vein that runs the full length of a leaf or segment.

Mobile Refers to a labellum that is loosely hinged at its point of attachment, therefore allowing movement.

Monocotyledon An angiosperm which has a single seed leaf and parallel leaf venation.

Monopodial A stem with a single main axis which grows forward at the tip (as opposed to sympodial).

Monotypic A genus with a single species.

Mycorrhiza The beneficial relationship between the roots of a vascular plant and fungi resulting in nutrient exchange.

Nectar A sweet fluid secreted from a nectary.

Node A point on a stem where leaves or bracts arise.

Osmophore A scent-producing gland.

Ovary The part of the flower that encloses the ovules and after fertilisation develops into a fruit.

Panicle A branched racemose inflorescence.
Pedicel The stem which supports a single flower in an inflorescence.
Peduncle The main axis of a compound inflorescence.
Pendent Hanging downwards.
Perianth A collective term for the sepals and petals of a flower.
Petal A segment of the inner perianth.
Petiole The stalk of a leaf.
Pollination The transfer of pollen from the anther to stigma of a flower.
Proliferous Producing buds or new plants vegetatively.
Pseudobulb Thickened stem of sympodial orchids.
Raceme Single unbranched inflorescence with stalked flowers.
Rachis The main axis of the lamina of a simple or compound leaf.
Reflexed Bent sharply backward or upward.
Resprouters Terrestrial orchids that die back to tubers to avoid hot, dry conditions.
Resupinate Orchid flowers right way up (column above, labellum below).
Rhizome An underground stem.
Rosette Group of basal leaves radiating in more or less a circle around a central axis.
Saprophyte A leafless or nearly leafless plant deriving sustenance from decaying wood and living in association with a symbiotic fungus.
Scape The peduncle and rachis of an inflorescence.
Sepal A segment of the calyx or outer whorl of the perianth.
Sessile Without a stalk.
Simple Undivided, in one piece, as in leaves.
Sinus The area between two lobes or segments.

Species A group of closely related plants with a common set of features that sets them apart from another species.

Spike Single unbranched inflorescence with sessile flowers.

Sterile bract A bract which does not subtend a pedicel or ovary.

Subgenus Taxonomic rank between genus and species.

Subspecies Taxonomic rank below species and above variety.

Sucker A shoot arising from the roots below ground level.

Sympodial A growth habit whereby each stem has limited growth and new shoots arise from the base of previous shoots.

Synonym Another name for the same taxon; either an alternative name valid in a different classification system or an invalid or incorrect name.

Taxon A term used to describe an individual within any taxonomic group.

Taxonomy The classification of plants or animals.

Tepal Applied when the sepals and petals are of similar shape and size.

Terete Slender and cylindrical.

Terrestrial Growing in the ground.

Tribe Taxonomic rank in classification used to denote a group of closely related genera.

Tuber A thickened or swollen root.

Umbel An inflorescence where the flowers radiate from a single point.

Whorl Three or more segments (bracts, leaves, flowers) in a circle at a node.

Variety Taxonomic rank below subspecies and above form.

FURTHER READING

Backhouse, G.N. (2018). *Spider Orchids the Genus* Caladenia *and its Relatives in Australia*, self-published by author, Melbourne.

Backhouse, G.N. (2019). *Bush Beauties: The Wild Orchids of Victoria, Australia.* Self-published by author, Melbourne.

Backhouse, G.N. (2023). *Guide to Native Orchids of Victoria.* CSIRO Publishing, Melbourne.

Backhouse, G.N., and Jeanes, J. (1995). *The Orchids of Victoria.* Miegunyah Press, Carlton, Victoria.

Bates, R., and Weber, J.Z. (1990). *Orchids of South Australia.* Government Printer, Adelaide.

Brown, A.P., Dundas, P., Dixon, K.W., and Hopper, S.D. (2008). *Orchids of Western Australia.* University of Western Australia Press, Crawley.

Brown, A.P., Dixon, K.W., French, C.J., and Brockman, G. (2013). *Field Guide to the Orchids of Western Australia.* Simon Neville Publications, York.

Brown, A. (2022). *The Complete Orchids of Western Australia.* Vols. 1 and 2. Self-published by author.

Brundrett, M. (2014). *Identification and Ecology of Southwest Australian Orchids: A User-friendly Guide.* Western Australian Naturalists Club, Perth.

Cady, L., and Rotherham, E.R. (1970), *Australian Native Orchids in Colour.* A.H. & A.W. Reed, Sydney.

Clements, M.A. (1978). Catalogue of Australian Orchidaceae. *Australian Orchid Research* 1–160.

Copeland, L.M., and Backhouse, G.N. (2022). *Guide to Native Orchids of NSW and ACT.* CSIRO Publishing, Melbourne.

FURTHER READING

Dockrill, A.W. (1967). *Australasian Sarcanthinae.* Australasian Native Orchid Society, Chipping Norton.

Dockrill, A.W. (1992). *Australian Indigenous Orchids*, Vols. 1 and 2. Surrey Beatty and Sons, Chipping Norton.

Hoffman, N., Brown, A.P., and Brown, J. (2019). *Orchids of Southwest Australia* (Fourth Edition). Self-published by author, Perth.

Jones, D.L. (2024). *A Complete Guide to Native Orchids of Australia.* Revised Third Edition. Reed New Holland, Sydney.

Jones, D.L. (2024). *A Field Guide to Australian Orchids: Epiphytes.* Revised Third Edition. Reed New Holland, Sydney.

Jones, D.L., Hopley, T., Duffy, S.M., Richards, K.J., Clements, M.A., and Zhang, X. (2006). *Australian Orchid Genera and Identification System.* CSIRO Publishing, Melbourne.

Jones, D.L., Hopley, T., and Duffy. S.M. (2010). *Australian Tropical Rainforest Orchids.* CSIRO Publishing, Melbourne.

Lavarack, P.S., and Gray, B. (1985). *Tropical Orchids of Australia*, Thomas Nelson, Melbourne.

Nicholls, W.H. (1969). *Orchids of Australia: Complete Edition* (1969). Edited by D.L. Jones and T.B. Muir. Thomas Nelson, Melbourne.

Niejalke, J., and Bates, R. (2022). *Native Orchids of South Australia.* Self-published by author, Pinnaroo.

Upton, W. (1989). *Dendrobium Orchids of Australia.* Houghton Mifflin Australia, Melbourne.

Upton, W. (1992). *Sarcochilus Orchids of Australia.* Double U Orchids, Gosford, NSW.

INDEX

INDEX

INDEX

INDEX

Other titles in the **Reed Concise Guides** series:

Animals of Australia
Ken Stepnell
ISBN 978 1 92151 754 9

Beetles of Australia
Paul Zborowski
ISBN 978 1 76079 611 2

Birds of Australia
Ken Stepnell
ISBN 978 1 92151 753 2

Butterflies of Australia
Paul Zborowski
ISBN 978 1 92554 694 1

Ferns of Australia
David L Jones
ISBN 978 1 76079 634 1

Frogs of Australia
Marion Anstis
ISBN 978 1 92151 790 7

Insects of Australia
Paul Zborowski
ISBN 978 1 92554 644 6

Lilies of Australia
David L Jones
ISBN 978 1 76079 617 4

Lizards of Australia
Steve K Wilson
ISBN 978 1 92554 657 6

Sea Fishes of Australia
Nigel Marsh
ISBN 978 1 76079 631 0

Snakes of Australia
Gerry Swan
ISBN 978 1 92151 789 1

Spiders of Australia
Volker W Framenau and Melissa L Thomas
ISBN 978 1 92554 603 3

Trees of Australia
David L Jones
ISBN 978 1 92554 688 0

Wild Flowers of Australia
Ken Stepnell
ISBN 978 1 92151 755 6

For details of these books and hundreds of other Natural History titles see **newhollandpublishers.com**